Burton Hobson

Catalogue of
SCANDINAVIAN
COINS

Gold, silver and minor coins
since 1534 with their valuations

STERLING
PUBLISHING CO., INC.   NEW YORK

Distributed by WARD LOCK, Ltd., London & Sydney

Books by Burton Hobson

Catalogue of Scandinavian Coins

Coin Collecting as a Hobby

Coin Identifier

Getting Started in Coin Collecting

Hidden Values in Coins

Copyright © 1970
by PRESIDENT COIN CORP.
4 Warwick Place, Port Washington, N.Y. 11050
British edition published by Oak Tree Press Co., Ltd.
Distributed in Great Britain and the Commonwealth by
Ward Lock, Ltd., 116 Baker Street, London W1
Manufactured in the United States of America
All rights reserved
Library of Congress Catalog Card No.: 79–90813
ISBN 0- 8069–6022 –1   UK 7061 2229 1
6023–X

CONTENTS

DENMARK 5

NORWAY 53

SWEDEN 71

FINLAND 123

ABOUT THIS BOOK

Starting with the early 1500's, this book lists every major coin by type issued by Denmark, Norway, Sweden and Finland.

For each country the coins have been arranged by reign (the monarch's names are spelled as in the language of their own country), in logical groupings, so that all coins of a given issue or with similar designs are found together. In the listings, each coin type has been assigned a number and its denomination, metal and years of issue given. An inclusive listing such as "1875–99" means that specimens bearing the first date and the last date have been reported. Coins with dates in between may or may not exist. A brief description of the obverse and reverse design of each coin is given except where the description of the coin above applies. Coins issued in such small quantity as to be considered patterns are not included.

The valuations shown are *estimates* of the prices that dealers charge for such coins from their stock. In arriving at these estimates, leading coin dealers were consulted, dealers' price lists from around the world and prices realized at auctions were studied. In many cases, very little price information was available and in other instances, prices realized for the same type of coin varied a great deal. Firm market values for Scandinavian coins do not exist as they do for Lincoln head cents or Queen Victoria halfpennies. In spite of the difficulties of the task, valuations have been included (in most cases for two conditions) with the idea that some indication of price is better than no information at all.

CONVERSION TABLE
U.S. Dollars into British Pounds

U.S. $	£ @ $2.40			£ @ $2.80			U.S. $	£ @ $2.40			£ @ $2.80		
	£	s.	d.	£	s.	d.		£	s.	d.	£	s.	d.
6.00	2	10	–	2	3	–	92.50	38	11	–	33	1	–
7.50	3	2	6	2	13	6	95.00	39	11	6	33	18	6
10.00	4	3	–	3	11	6	97.50	40	12	6	34	16	6
12.50	5	4	–	4	9	–	100.00	41	13	6	35	14	6
15.00	6	5	–	5	7	6	105.00	43	15	–	37	10	–
17.50	7	6	–	6	5	–	110.00	45	16	6	39	6	–
20.00	8	6	6	7	3	–	115.00	47	19	6	41	1	6
22.50	9	7	6	8	1	–	120.00	50	–	–	42	17	–
25.00	10	8	6	8	18	6	125.00	52	1	6	44	13	–
27.50	11	9	–	9	16	6	130.00	54	3	6	46	8	6
30.00	12	10	–	10	14	–	135.00	56	5	–	48	4	–
32.50	13	11	–	11	12	–	140.00	58	6	6	50	–	–
35.00	14	11	6	12	10	–	145.00	60	8	6	51	16	–
37.50	15	12	6	13	8	–	150.00	62	10	–	53	11	6
40.00	16	13	6	14	6	–	155.00	64	11	6	55	7	–
42.50	17	14	–	15	3	6	160.00	66	13	6	57	3	–
45.00	18	15	–	16	1	6	165.00	68	15	–	58	18	6
47.50	19	16	–	16	19	–	170.00	70	16	6	60	14	–
50.00	20	16	6	17	17	–	175.00	72	18	6	62	10	–
52.50	21	17	6	18	15	–	180.00	75	–	–	65	6	–
55.00	22	18	6	19	13	–	185.00	77	1	6	66	1	6
57.50	23	19	–	20	11	–	190.00	79	3	6	67	17	–
60.00	25	–	–	21	8	6	195.00	85	5	–	69	13	–
62.50	26	1	–	22	6	6	200.00	83	6	6	71	8	6
65.00	27	1	6	23	4	–	210.00	87	10	–	75	–	–
67.50	28	2	6	24	2	–	225.00	93	15	–	80	7	–
70.00	29	3	6	25	–	–	235.00	97	19	6	83	18	6
72.50	30	4	–	25	18	–	250.00	104	3	6	89	6	–
75.00	31	5	–	26	16	–	260.00	108	6	6	92	17	–
77.50	32	6	–	27	13	6	275.00	114	11	6	98	4	–
80.00	33	6	6	28	11	6	285.00	118	15	–	101	16	–
82.50	34	7	6	29	9	–	300.00	125	–	–	107	3	–
85.00	35	8	6	30	7	–	400.00	166	13	6	142	17	–
87.50	36	9	–	31	5	–	500.00	208	6	6	178	11	6
90.00	37	10	–	32	3	–	1,000.00	416	13	6	357	3	–

DENMARK

CHRISTIAN III 1534-59

		Fine	Ext. Fine
1.	1 Gulden—Joachimsdaler (S) 1537, 45, 47. Half-length figure of King. Rev. Quartered arms	150–	300–
2.	½ Gulden (S) 1537, 47	75–	175–

		Fine	Ext. Fine
* 3.	1 Mark (S) 1541–55. Arms—three lions. Rev. Value	40–	75–
4.	8 Skillings (S) 1541, 44	15–	40–
5.	4 Skillings (S) 1541–54	10–	30–
6.	2 Skillings (S) 1557–59	8.50	20–
* 7.	1 Skilling (S) 1542–58	7.50	17.50

* *Indicates coin or coins illustrated*

Denmark 5

			Fine	Ext. Fine
8.	1 Hvid (S) N.D. Arms—Oldenburg. Rev. Crowned monogram		10–	25–
9.	1 Penning (S) 1546. Arms—three lions. Rev. Value		20–	50–

10.	1 Guldgulden (G) 1557. Crowned head right. Rev. Quartered arms	1,000	2,500

FREDERIK II 1559–1588

*11.	3 Marks—1 speciedaler (S) 1560, 63. Arms—three lions. Rev. Value	100–	200–
12.	1 Mark (S) 1559–63, 82	15–	35–
13.	8 Skillings (S) 1560–63, 82–85	12.50	25–
14.	2 Skillings (S) 1559–63, 82–85	10–	20–
*15.	1 Skilling (S) 1562, 63, 82, 83	8.50	17.50

16.	1 Ducat, gulden or krone (G) 1564. Crowned monogram. Rev. Value (klippe)	1,500–	2,750–

		Fine	Ext. Fine
*17.	2 Marks (S) 1563, 64. Crowned monogram. Rev. Value (klippe)	75–	125–
18.	1 Mark (S) 1563–65 (klippe)	50–	95–
19.	4 Skillings (S) 1563 (klippe)	35–	65–
*20.	2 Skillings (S) 1564–66. Arms. Rev. Value (klippe)	25–	50–

Note: These "clipped" coins were emergency issues produced during the Seven Years War.

21.	1 Speciedaler (S) 1572. Bust left. Rev. Quartered arms	100–	250–

*22.	8 Skillings (S) 1579. Crowned monogram. Rev. Value	10–	20–
23.	1 Skilling (S) 1579	10–	20–
*24.	1 Hvid (S) 1579–83. Arms (Oldenburg). Rev. Crowned monogram	6–	15–

Note: A series of seven gold pieces dated 1584 in denominations of various foreign coins were presentation pieces not intended for circulation.

REGNA FIRMAT PIETAS—*Piety Strengthens Kingly Rule*

			Fine	Ext. Fine
25.	1 Portugaloser (G) 1591, 92. Cross. Rev. Quartered arms		1,750–	2,500–
26.	¼ Portugaloser (G) 1592, 93		600–	1,000–

		Fine	Ext. Fine
27.	1 Speciedaler (S) 1596. Crowned bust right. Rev. Arms—three lions (coronation)	200–	350–
28.	1 Speciedaler (S) 1597. Rev. Quartered arms (wedding)	200–	350–

		Fine	Ext. Fine
*29.	4 Marks—1 speciedaler (S) 1596. Arms—three lions. Rev. Value	60–	200–
30.	2 Marks (S) 1604	15–	45–

		Fine	Ext. Fine
31.	24 Skillings (S) 1624	5–	12.50
32.	1 Mark (S) 1596–1606	10–	20–
33.	16 Skillings (S) 1624, 25	5–	15–
34.	8 Skillings (S) 1596, 1606	8.50	20–
35.	6 Skillings (S) 1627–29	5–	10–
36.	4 Skillings (S) 1596–1619	4–	8.50
37.	2 Skillings (S) 1594–1648	3–	7.50
* 38.	1 Skilling (S) 1595–1648	4.50	10–

| 39. | 1 Hvid (S) 1602–24. Cross. Rev. Crowned monogram | 4– | 8.50 |

Note: The last two coins were struck in very base silver, some specimens are almost pure copper.

| 40. | 2 Pennings (C) 1602. Crowned monogram. Rev. Value | 3.50 | 15– |

41.	8 Dalers (G) 1604. Crowned bust right. Rev. Value (square planchet)	Very rare
* 42.	6 Dalers (G) 1604 (square planchet)	Very rare
43.	4 Dalers (G) 1604 (square planchet)	Very rare

| 44. | 1 Portugaloser (G) N.D. King on horseback. Rev. Arms | 2,000– | 3,000– |

		Fine	Ext. Fine
45.	1 Double speciedaler-broad planchet (S) N.D. King on horseback. Rev. Quartered arms	200–	450–

46.	1 Liondaler (S) 1608. Knight in armor, arms on shield. Rev. Norwegian lion	Very rare

Note: Struck for trade with Netherlands, design similar to Dutch coin.

47.	1 Sovereign (G) 1608. King standing. Rev. Circle of shields	2,000–	3,000–
* 48.	1 Goldgulden (G) 1591–1611. King standing. Rev. Quartered arms	250–	400–
* 49.	1 Speciedaler (S) 1608–21. King standing. Rev. Circle of shields	50–	175–

		Fine	Ext. Fine
*50.	1 Rose noble (G) 1611–29. Crowned bust. Rev. Elephant	1,000–	2,000–
51.	½ Rose noble (G) 1611		Very rare
*52.	1 Goldgulden (G) 1604–32. Crowned bust. Rev. Arms	250–	400–

53.	1 Double speciedaler—broad planchet (S) N.D. Armored 2/3-length figure. Rev. King on horseback	175–	400–

54.	1 Double speciedaler—thick planchet (S) 1624–47. Crowned bust above tablet. Rev. Circle of shields	85–	250–
*55.	1 Speciedaler (S) 1624–47	50–	150–
56.	½ Speciedaler (S) 1624–46	30–	85–

			Fine	Ext. Fine
*57.	1 Mark (S) 1606–28. Crowned bust right. Rev. Value and arms		10–	35–
58.	8 Skillings (S) 1606–09		8.50	20–
59.	4 Skillings (S) 1606–09		5–	15–
60.	8 Skillings (S) 1630. Rev. Value		8.50	15–
61.	6 Skillings (S) 1628, 29		7.50	15–
*62.	1 Sosling (S) N.D. Crowned bust right. Rev. Arms		5–	10–

63.	1 Piaster (S) 1624. Arms. Rev. Crown	Very rare

Note: Struck for trade with the East Indies.

*64.	2 Goldkroner (G) 1619–48. Arms. Rev. Crown	600–	1,000–
65.	1 Goldkrone (G) 1619	400–	600–
*66.	½ Goldkrone (G) 1619	200–	300–

67.	2 Goldkroner (G) 1628, 29. Crowned bust right. Rev. Crown	225–	450–

		Fine	Ext. Fine
*68.	2 Kroner—broad planchet (S) 1618–24. King standing. Rev. Crown	100–	250–
69.	1 Krone (S) 1618–24	25–	85–
*70.	½ Krone (S) 1618–24	20–	50–
71.	¼ Krone (S) 1618	12.50	35–
*72.	⅛ Krone (S) 1618	10–	27.50

		Fine	Ext. Fine
*73.	8 Skillings (S) 1619–21. Crown. Rev. Value	12.50	20–
74.	4 Skillings (S) 1619–21	8.50	15–
75.	2 Skillings (S) 1619–21	6–	12.50
76.	1 Skilling (S) 1619		Rare

		Fine	Ext. Fine
*77.	12 Skillings (S) 1622, 23. Arms. Rev. Monogram	7.50	12.50
78.	6 Skillings (S) 1622	3–	7.50
79.	4 Skillings (S) 1630, 32. Rev. Value	8.50	20–

		Fine	Ext. Fine
*80.	12 Skillings (S) 1624, 25. Crowned monogram. Rev. Value	7.50	12.50
81.	8 Skillings (S) 1622–25	6–	10–
82.	1 Skilling (S) 1619–23	2.50	7.50

83.	1 Sosling (C) 1624. Crowned bust right. Rev. Value	4–	10–

*84.	1 Ducat (G) 1644–48. King standing. Rev. Latin and Hebrew inscription, "Justus Jehova Judex"—*The Lord Is a Righteous Judge*	200–	350–
85.	½ Ducat (G) 1644–46	85–	200–
86.	¼ Ducat (G) 1646, 47	65–	175–

*87.	2 Marks (S) 1644–47. Crowned monogram. Rev. Inscription, "Justus Jehova Judex"	20–	45–
*88.	16 Skillings—1 mark (S) 1644–47	12.50	32.50
89.	4 Skillings (S) 1644, 45	8.50	20–

*90.	½ Ducat (G) 1647. King standing. Rev. Pair of spectacles and inscription, "Videmira Domi"—*See the Wonders of the Lord*		Very rare
91.	½ Ducat (G) 1647. Crowned monogram		Very rare

FREDERIK III 1648–1670

DOMINUS PROVIDEBIT—*The Lord Will Provide*

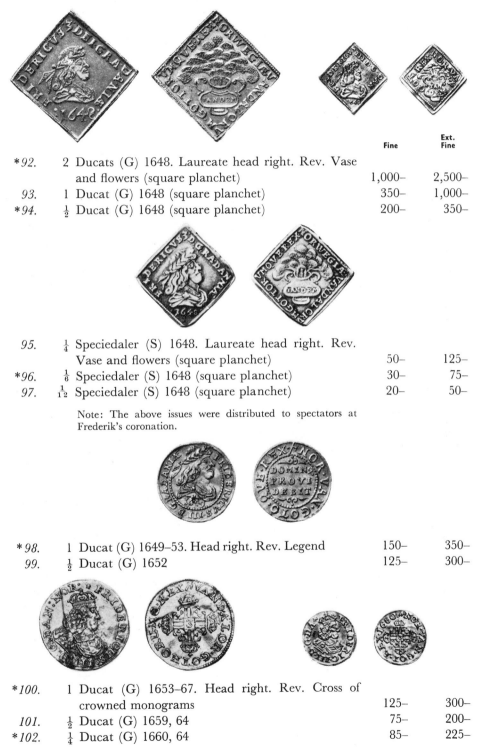

		Fine	Ext. Fine
*92.	2 Ducats (G) 1648. Laureate head right. Rev. Vase and flowers (square planchet)	1,000–	2,500–
93.	1 Ducat (G) 1648 (square planchet)	350–	1,000–
*94.	½ Ducat (G) 1648 (square planchet)	200–	350–
95.	¼ Speciedaler (S) 1648. Laureate head right. Rev. Vase and flowers (square planchet)	50–	125–
*96.	⅙ Speciedaler (S) 1648 (square planchet)	30–	75–
97.	1/12 Speciedaler (S) 1648 (square planchet)	20–	50–

Note: The above issues were distributed to spectators at Frederik's coronation.

*98.	1 Ducat (G) 1649–53. Head right. Rev. Legend	150–	350–
99.	½ Ducat (G) 1652	125–	300–
*100.	1 Ducat (G) 1653–67. Head right. Rev. Cross of crowned monograms	125–	300–
101.	½ Ducat (G) 1659, 64	75–	200–
*102.	¼ Ducat (G) 1660, 64	85–	225–

Denmark
15

		Fine	Ext. Fine
103.	1 Double speciedaler—thick planchet (S) 1649–61. Crowned bust right. Rev. Circle of shields	175–	350–
*104.	1 Speciedaler (S) 1649–62	100–	250–

| 105. | 2 Ducats (S) 1657–67. Crowned bust right. Rev. Ship | 500– | 1,000– |
| 106. | 2 Ducats (G) 1662, 63. Crowned bust right. Rev. Quartered arms | 600– | 1,000– |

| 107. | 1 Ducat (G) 1669, 70. Crowned bust right. Rev. Three shields | 500– | 1,000– |

| 108. | 1 Double speciedaler—broad planchet (S) 1669. Laureate bust right. Rev. Three shields, circle of arms | 200– | 450– |
| 109. | 8 Skillings (S) 1669. Crowned bust right. Rev. Three shields | 7.50 | 20– |

		Fine	Ext. Fine
110.	1 Double speciedaler—thick planchet (S) 1665–69. Laureate bust right. Rev. Arms	150–	350–
111.	1 Speciedaler (S) 1664–69	60–	175–

112.	2 Ducats—thick planchet (G) N.D. Laureate head right. Rev. Crown and orb between scepter and sword	275–	450–
113.	2 Ducats (G) 1670. Laureate head right. Rev. Cross of monograms	600–	1,250–

114.	1 Goldkrone (G) 1655–60. Arms. Rev. Crown	200–	450–

115.	18 Marks—1 goldkrone (G) 1666, 68. Laureate head right. Rev. Crown	500–	950–

Denmark 17

		Fine	Ext. Fine
116.	1 Double kroner—thick planchet (S) 1651. Crowned bust right. Rev. Crown	250–	450–
117.	1 Krone (S) 1651	85–	225–
118.	½ Krone (S) 1651	35–	100–

119.	1 Sosling (C) 1651. Crowned monogram. Rev. Value	10–	25–
120.	1 Hvid (C) 1651. Rev. Cross	6–	15–

121.	6 Marks—½ ducat—thick planchet (G) 1669. Crowned monogram. Rev. Value	275–	500–
122.	3 Marks—¼ ducat (G) 1665, 68	125–	300–
123.	¼ Ducat (G) 1670. Crowned monogram. Rev. Arms	100–	225–

124.	4 Marks—1 krone (S) 1652–70. Arms—three lions. Rev. Crowned monogram	40–	100–
125.	2 Marks (S) 1652–69	35–	125–
126.	1 Mark (S) 1668	50–	150–
127.	4 Skillings (S) 1665. Crowned monogram. Rev. Value	10–	25–
128.	2 Skillings (S) 1665, 66	8.50	15–

		Fine	Ext. Fine
129.	4 Skillings (S) 1667, 69. Arms. Rev. Value	7.50	20–
*130.	2 Skillings (S) 1648–70	6–	15–
131.	1 Skilling (S) 1648–67	5–	10–

		Fine	Ext. Fine
132.	1 Double krone—thick planchet (S) 1659. Monogram and Ebenezer stone. Rev. Hand of God striking the arm of Swedish king reaching for Danish crown (Swedish attack on Copenhagen repulsed)	100–	275–
*133.	1 Krone (S) 1659	40–	125–

		Fine	Ext. Fine
134.	1 Krone (S) 1666. Laureate bust. Rev. Crown	65–	150–
135.	2 Marks (S) 1665–67	35–	95–
136.	1 Mark (S) 1666	15–	50–

PIETATE ET IUSTITIA—*Piety and Justice*

	Fine	Ext. Fine
137. 1 Speciedaler (S) N.D. (1670). Armored bust. Rev. Armored bust of Frederik III (accession to throne)		Very rare

		Fine	Ext. Fine
138.	2 Ducats (G) 1670. Laureate bust right. Rev. Crowned monograms	400–	1,000–
*139.	½ Ducat (G) 1675	150–	400–

		Fine	Ext. Fine
140.	1 Speciedaler (S) 1671–83. Armored bust right. Rev. Crowned monogram	100–	250–
141.	1 Speciedaler (S) 1670, 74, 91. Rev. Circle of shields, arms	100–	250–

		Fine	Ext. Fine
142.	2 Ducats (G) 1671–74. Laureate bust right. Rev. Three shields	250–	450–

| *143.* | 3 Marks—¼ ducat (G) 1675. Crowned monograms. Rev. Value | 125– | 300– |

144.	4 Marks—1 krone (S) 1671–82. Crowned monogram. Rev. Arms	45–	125–
145.	2 Marks (S) 1671–82	15–	40–
146.	1 Mark (S) 1672, 76. Rev. Value	6–	15–
147.	8 Skillings (S) 1672–97	4–	10–

148.	4 Skillings (S) 1677–94. Rev. Arms	3–	7.50
149.	2 Skillings (S) 1676–94. Arms. Rev. Value	4–	8.50
150.	1 Skilling (S) 1676–94	3–	6–

		Fine	Ext. Fine
151.	2 Ducats (G) 1673. Elephant. Rev. Crowned monogram	600–	1,000–
152.	1 Ducat (G) N.D. King on horseback. Rev. Crowned monograms	175–	350–

153.	2 Kroner (S) 1675. King on horseback. Rev. Arms	85–	200–

154.	1 Speciedaler (S) 1675. Crowned half-length figure with scepter and orb. Rev. Crowned monograms	100–	275–

155.	1 Krone (S) 1680. Bust of King on pedestal. Rev. Arms	100	225–

		Fine	Ext. Fine
156.	3 Marks—¼ ducat (G) 1676. Laureate head right. Rev. Value	125–	250–
157.	1 Ducat (G) 1682. Bust right. Rev. Fortress	225–	500–

		Fine	Ext. Fine
158.	2 Ducats (G) 1687. Bust right. Rev. Arms in circle of shields	450–	1,500–
*159.	1 Ducat (G) 1687	350–	1,250–

		Fine	Ext. Fine
*160.	1 Speciedaler (S) 1687–93. Draped bust right. Rev. Arms in circle of shields	125–	350–
161.	½ Speciedaler (S) 1693	65–	150–

Note: This issue was struck at the Kongsberg, Norway mint (HCM mintmaster's mark). Only issues with distinctive Norwegian designs are catalogued under Norway.

		Fine	Ext. Fine
162.	1 Speciedaler (S) 1693–96. Rev. Arms	150–	400–

Note: This issue was struck at the Kongsberg, Norway mint (HCM mintmaster's mark). Only issues with distinctive Norwegian designs are catalogued under Norway.

		Fine	Ext. Fine
163.	2 Ducats—thick planchet (G) 1688. Helmeted bust right. Rev. Fort Christiansborg in Guinea (now in the African state of Ghana)	1,000–	2,000–
*164.	1 Ducat (G) 1688	650–	1,250–
165.	2 Ducats—thick planchet (G) 1691. Bust right. Rev. Arms	450–	1,000–
*166.	1 Ducat (G) 1681–92	125–	350–

		Fine	Ext. Fine
*167.	4 Marks—1 krone (S) 1690. Half-length armored bust right. Rev. Quartered arms	50–	125–
168.	2 Marks (S) 1690	30–	65–

		Fine	Ext. Fine
*169.	1 Ducat (G) 1691. Crowned double monogram. Rev. Arms	150–	300–
*170.	4 Marks—1 krone (S) 1684–94. Crowned double monogram. Rev. Arms	17.50	40–
171.	2 Marks (S) 1684–96	10–	20–
172.	1 Mark (S) 1685–92	7.50	15–

		Fine	Ext. Fine
*173.	2 Skillings (S) 1686. Rev. Value	5–	10–
174.	1 Skilling (S) 1686–99	4–	7.50
175.	½ Skilling (S) 1686	3–	7.50
*176.	1 Hvid (S) 1686. Crowned monogram. Rev. Value	4–	8.50

		Fine	Ext. Fine
177.	2 Ducats (G) 1692. Bust right. Rev. Crowned monograms	500–	1,250–
*178.	1 Ducat (G) 1672–96	150–	350–

		Fine	Ext. Fine
179.	2 Ducats (G) 1693. Bust right. Rev. Crown	300–	600–
*180.	1 Ducat (G) 1693	175–	350–
181.	½ Ducat (G) 1694, 96	100–	200–

		Fine	Ext. Fine
*182.	1 Krone (S) 1693–99. Bust right. Rev. Crown	10–	20–
183.	2 Marks (S) 1699	8.50	15–
184.	1 Mark (S) 1693–99	7.50	12.50
*185.	8 Skillings (S) 1693, 95	6–	12.50
186.	4 Skillings (S) 1696	5–	10–
187.	2 Skillings (S) 1693	3.50	7.50
*188.	½ Skilling (C) 1693–96	4–	7.50

		Fine	Ext. Fine
189.	1 Ducat (G) 1696. N.D. King on horseback. Rev. Arms	275–	600–
190.	1 Ducat (G) 1699. Head right. Rev. Ship	250–	600–

191. 1 Ducat (G) N.D. Pyramid. Rev. View of Copenhagen
harbor   250–   600–

Note: Memorial issue struck at time of King's death.

FREDERIK IV 1699–1730

DOMINUS MIHI ADIUTOR—*The Lord Is My Helper*

192.	1 Ducat (G) 1699. Bust right. Rev. Bust right of Christian V (accession to throne)	350–	750–
193.	1 Triple kroner—thick planchet (S) 1699	225–	450–

			Fine	Ext. Fine
194.	2 Ducats (G) 1701, 04. Armored bust right. Rev. Crowned monograms		450–	1,000–
*195.	1 Ducat (G) 1700		200–	375–
*196.	1 Ducat (G) N.D. King on horseback to left. Rev. Crowned monograms		200–	350–

			Fine	Ext. Fine
*197.	2 Ducats (G) 1701, 04. Armored Bust right. Rev. Fort Christianborg		1,500–	2,500–
198.	1 Ducat (G) 1704–25		450–	750–
199.	5 Ducats (G) 1704. Armored bust right. Rev. Ship		1,750–	3,000–
*200.	2 Ducats (G) 1708		1,250–	2,000–
201.	1 Ducat (G) 1701		500–	850–

Note: The 1708 2-ducat piece with SOC IND OCC was struck for the Danish West Indies Company.

202.   1 Reisedaler (S) 1704. Armored bust right. Rev. Norwegian lion (see Norway #46)

			Fine	Ext. Fine
203.	2 Ducats (G) 1708. Armored bust right. Rev. Arms and monograms		450–	750–
*204.	1 Ducat (G) 1708, 09		150–	300–
*205.	1 Krone (S) 1699–1702. Armored bust right. Rev. Arms and monograms		65–	225–
206.	2 Marks (S) 1700		20–	50–

Note: Specimens of this issue with crossed hammers mint mark were struck at the Kongsberg, Norway mint. Only coins with distinctive Norwegian designs are catalogued under Norway.

Denmark   **27**

		Fine	Ext. Fine

*207. 1 Ducat (G) 1709–26. Armored bust right. Rev.
Arms — 150– / 300–

208. 1 Speciedaler (S) 1704. Armored bust right. Rev.
Arms — 85– / 225–

209. 1 Ducat (G) 1711. King on horseback to right. Rev.
Arms — 200– / 350–

210. 1 Krone (S) 1711, 23. King on horseback. Rev. Arms — 50– / 175–

211. 2 Rixdalers—1 courant ducat (G) 1714–16. Head.
Rev. Crown — 300– / 500–

*212. 1 Rixdaler—$\frac{1}{2}$ courant ducat (G) 1715 — 150– / 275–

*213. 16 Skillings—1 mark (S) 1713–17. Head right. Rev.
Value — 5– / 17.50

214. 12 Skillings (S) 1721. Rev. Arms — 12.50 / 35–

*215. 8 Skillings (S) 1700–15. Rev. Crown — 2.50 / 8.50

216. 8 Skillings (S) 1729, 30. Rev. Value — 3.50 / 10–

		Fine	Ext. Fine
217.	4 Marks—1 krone (S) 1724, 26. Crowned monograms. Rev. Crown	65–	250–
*218.	1 Krone (S) 1725, 26. Crowned monograms. Rev. Arms	37.50	150–
219.	2 Marks (S) 1725, 26	6–	20–

		Fine	Ext. Fine
*220.	12 Skillings (S) 1710–24. Crowned monograms. Rev. Value	6–	12.50
221.	12 Skillings (S) 1716–22. Rev. Arms	6–	12.50
222.	8 Skillings (S) 1727, 28. Rev. Value	5–	10–
223.	4 Skillings (S) 1727–30. Rev. Arms	4–	8.50
224.	2 Skillings (S) 1711–19. Rev. Value	3–	5–
225.	2 Skillings (S) 1714–16. Rev. Arms	3.50	6.50
226.	1 Skilling (S) 1700–21. Rev. Value	1.50	3–
*227.	1 Skilling (S) 1720–23. Rev. Arms	2–	4.50
*228.	½ Skilling (C) 1719. Rev. Value	3–	5–

		Fine	Ext. Fine
229.	1 Triple kroner—broad planchet (S) 1726. Bust right. Rev. Arms in circle of shields	400–	750–

Note: Many issues of this reign were struck at Kongsberg, Norway (crossed hammers mintmark) as well as at the mints in Denmark proper. Only issues with distinctive Norwegian designs are catalogued under Norway.

CHRISTIAN VI 1730–46

DEO ET POPVLO—*For God and the People*

			Fine	Ext. Fine
230.	1 Ducat (G) 1730, 38, 40. Crowned monograms. Rev. Fort Christianborg		200–	350–
231.	1 Ducat (G) 1732. Bust right. Rev. Quartered arms		300–	500–

232.	4 Marks—1 krone (S) 1731, 32. Armored bust right. Rev. Crown		65–	175–

*233.	24 Skillings (S) 1731, 32. Rev. Arms		7.50	20–
*234.	24 Skillings (S) 1732–43. Crowned monograms. Rev. Arms		5–	12.50
235.	1 Skilling (S) 1735, 46. Rev. Value		1.50	3.50

236.	½ Skilling (C) 1745		2–	5–
237.	6 Marks—1 reisedaler (S) 1732, 33. Armored bust right. Rev. Norwegian lion (see Norway #49)			

PRUDENTIA ET CONSTANTIA—*Wisdom and Steadfastness*

			Fine	Ext. Fine
238.	1 Ducat (G) N.D. (1746). Bust right. Rev. Bust right of Christian VI (accession to throne)		75–	200–
239.	1 Triple kroner—thick planchet (S) N.D. (1746)		200–	375–

240.	1 Ducat (G) 1746. Bust right. Rev. Arms		350–	750–
241.	1 Ducat (G) 1746. Rev. Galley and inscription, "Ex Auro Sinico"—*From Chinese Gold*		125–	275–

242.	1 Ducat (G) 1746. Head right. Rev. Ship and Fort Christianborg		125–	275–
243.	1 Ducat (G) 1747. King standing. Rev. Fort Christianborg		125–	275–

Note: Above two issues struck of African gold from Guinea.

244.	1 Ducat (G) 1747. King standing. Rev. Arms		200–	350–
245.	1 Ducat (G) 1747. Bust right. Rev. Arms		275–	500–

		Fine	Ext. Fine
246.	1 Double speciedaler—thick planchet (S) 1747. King standing below canopy. Rev. Wild men supporting arms (coronation)	200–	375–
*247.	1 Speciedaler (S) 1747	50–	125–

248.	1 Double kroner—thick planchet (S) 1747. Bust right. Rev. Crown	100–	250–
*249.	1 Krone (S) 1747	30–	100–

250.	1 Ducat (G) 1748. King on galloping horse. Rev. Crowned monograms	500–	1,000–
251.	1 Ducat (G) 1749. King on horseback. Rev. Arms	100–	200–

Note: The 1749 ducat with DWC on a ribbon below the trident was struck for the Danish West Indies Company.

252.	1 Ducat (G) 1753–56. Head right. Rev. Ship	125–	250–
253.	1 Ducat (G) 1758. Head right. Rev. Arms and inscription, "Ebenezer"	125–	250–

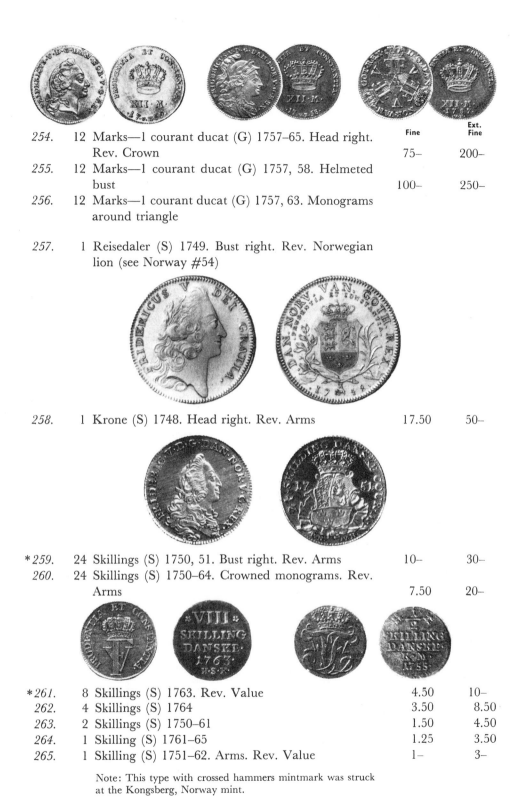

		Fine	Ext. Fine
254.	12 Marks—1 courant ducat (G) 1757–65. Head right. Rev. Crown	75–	200–
255.	12 Marks—1 courant ducat (G) 1757, 58. Helmeted bust	100–	250–
256.	12 Marks—1 courant ducat (G) 1757, 63. Monograms around triangle		
257.	1 Reisedaler (S) 1749. Bust right. Rev. Norwegian lion (see Norway #54)		
258.	1 Krone (S) 1748. Head right. Rev. Arms	17.50	50–
*259.	24 Skillings (S) 1750, 51. Bust right. Rev. Arms	10–	30–
260.	24 Skillings (S) 1750–64. Crowned monograms. Rev. Arms	7.50	20–
*261.	8 Skillings (S) 1763. Rev. Value	4.50	10–
262.	4 Skillings (S) 1764	3.50	8.50
263.	2 Skillings (S) 1750–61	1.50	4.50
264.	1 Skilling (S) 1761–65	1.25	3.50
265.	1 Skilling (S) 1751–62. Arms. Rev. Value	1–	3–

Note: This type with crossed hammers mintmark was struck at the Kongsberg, Norway mint.

| *266. | ½ Skilling (C) 1751–62. Crowned monograms. Rev. Value | 1.50 | 3.50 |

		Fine	Ext. Fine
267.	1 Speciedaler (S) 1764, 65. Head right. Rev. Arms	50–	150–

CHRISTIAN VII 1766–1808

GLORIA EX AMORE PATRIAE—*Glory from Love of Country*

| *268.* | 1 Speciedaler (S) 1769. Bust. Rev. Arms in ribbon (Order of the Elephant) | 200– | 350– |

269.	1 Speciedaler (S) 1769. Crowned monograms. Rev. Type of # 268	30–	60–
270.	½ Speciedaler (S) 1769	10–	25–
271.	¼ Speciedaler (S) 1769	7.50	15–

* 269. refers to entry 269.

		Fine	Ext. Fine
*272.	1 Courant ducat (G) 1771. Bust. Rev. "29 Januarii" in wreath (King's birthday)	300–	500–
*273.	1 Krone (S) 1771	20–	50–
274.	½ Krone (S) 1771	12.50	30–

275.	1 Ducat (G) 1771, 1791–1802, Wild man. Rev. Legend on tablet	150–	300–

Note: Similar to design of Holy Roman Empire trade ducats.

276.	1 Piaster (S) 1771, 77. Arms. Rev. Pillars and globes	Very rare

Note: Copied from Spanish-American 8 reales but Danish and Norwegian arms on globes. Struck for trade with India and China.

277.	1 Albert daler (S) 1781–96. Wild man supporting Danish arms. Rev. Crowned Norwegian arms	100–	250–

Note: Copied from Dutch rijksdaler of Austrian Archduke Albert, 1598–1621. Struck for Baltic trade.

		Fine	Ext. Fine
*278.	1 Speciedaler (S) 1771–85. Crowned monograms. Rev. Arms in wreath	15–	40–
279.	½ Speciedaler (S) 1776–86	10–	25–
280.	24 Skillings (S) 1767, 1778–83. Crowned monogram. Rev. Arms	4–	10–
281.	8 Skillings (S) 1778–95	2–	6–
282.	4 Skillings (S) 1778, 88	2–	6–
*283.	2 Skillings (S) 1778–88	1–	4.50

		Fine	Ext. Fine
284.	8 Skillings (S) 1773–83. Crowned monogram. Rev. Value	2–	6–
*285.	4 Skillings (S) 1783	1.50	5–
286.	1 Skilling (S) 1768–70. Crowned monograms. Rev. Value	1.50	4.50

		Fine	Ext. Fine
*287.	1 Skilling (C) 1771, 79. Crowned monograms. Rev. Value	.50	2.50
288.	½ Skilling (C) 1771. Crowned monogram	.75	3–

		Fine	Ext. Fine
289.	1 Christian d'or (G) N.D., 1775. Head right. Rev. Monograms	300–	450–

		Fine	Ext. Fine
290.	32 Skillings (S) 1775. Head left. Rev. Arms	10–	25–
291.	12 Marks—1 courant ducat (G) 1781–85. Head right. Rev. Crown	175–	300–
292.	1 Reisedaler (S) 1788. Bust right. Rev. Norwegian lion (see Norway #61)		

*293.	1 Speciedaler (S) 1791–1801. Head right. Rev. Arms	15–	40–
294.	⅔ Speciedaler (S) 1795, 96	12.50	30–
295.	⅓ Speciedaler (S) 1795–1803	10–	20–

296.	⅕ Speciedaler—¼ courant rigsdaler (S) 1796–1803. Crowned monogram. Rev. Value	5–	10–
*297.	1/15 Speciedaler—1/12 courant rigsdaler (S) 1795–1802. Arms. Rev. Value	2–	6–

*298.	4 Skillings (S) 1807. Crowned monogram, no legend. Rev. Value	1–	3.50
299.	2 Skillings (S) 1800–07	.75	2.50
300.	1 Skilling (S) 1779–82	1–	3–

Note: Many issues of this reign were struck at Kongsberg, Norway (crossed hammers mintmark) as well as at the mints in Denmark proper. Only issues with distinctive Norwegian designs are catalogued under Norway.

FREDERIK VI 1808–39

INFLATION COINAGE

		Fine	Ext. Fine
301.	1/6 Courant rigsdaler (S) 1808. Crowned monogram. Rev. Inscription—*Voluntary Offering to the Fatherland*	2–	5–

Note: Struck from silver plate turned in by citizens.

*302.	8 Skillings (S) 1809. Crowned monogram. Rev. Value	2.50	6–
303.	4 Skillings (S) 1809	1–	2.50
*304.	1 Skilling (S) 1808, 09	.75	2–

305.	4 Skillings (C) 1809. Crowned monogram. Rev. Value	1.50	4–
*306.	2 Skillings (C) 1810	.50	1.50
307.	1 Skilling (C) 1809, 12 (smaller planchet)	.75	2–

Note: Some of these issues were struck from copper taken from the roof of the Church of Our Lady in Copenhagen. Due to inflation, the 1810 2-skilling coins are the same size as the 1809 1-skilling pieces. Most of the above issues were struck at Kongsberg, Norway (crossed hammers mintmark). Only issues with distinctive Norwegian designs are catalogued under Norway.

308.	12 Skillings (C) 1812. Head. Rev. Arms	1.50	3.50

Note: Frequently struck over 1771 1-skilling coins.

309.	3 Skillings (C) 1812		.75
310.	2 Skillings (C) 1809–11		.50

Note: Due to progressive inflation, the 1812 3-skilling coins are smaller than the 1809–11 2-skilling issues.

TOKEN COINAGE

		Fine	Ext. Fine
311.	1 Rigsbank skilling (C) 1813. Head right. Rev. Value	.50	1.50

		Fine	Ext. Fine
*312.	16 Skillings rigsbanktegn—National Bank token (C) 1814. Quartered arms. Rev. Value	3–	7.50
313.	12 Skillings (C) 1813. Arms. (3 quarterings)	2–	4.50
*314.	6 Skillings (C) 1813	1.50	3–
315.	4 Skillings (C) 1815	1–	2.50
316.	3 Skillings (C) 1815	.75	1.75
*317.	2 Skillings (C) 1815	.50	

REGULAR COINAGE

		Very Fine	Unc.
318.	2 Frederik d'or (G) 1827 only 1 specimen known		
*319.	1 Frederik d'or (G) 1827	150–	350–
320.	2 Frederik d'or (G) 1828–36. Rev. Arms	450–	950–
* 321.	1 Frederik d'or (G) 1828–38	175–	400–
*322.	2 Frederik d'or (G) 1836–39. Head right. Rev. Wild men supporting arms	500–	1,000–

		Very Fine	Unc.
323.	1 Speciedaler (S) 1819. Head right. Rev. Arms (oval shield)	22.50	50–
324.	1 Speciedaler (S) 1820–39. Head right, side whiskers. Rev. Quartered arms	15–	37.50

*325.	1 Rigsbankdaler (S) 1813–19. Head right. Rev. Arms (square shield)	7.50	20–
326.	1 Rigsbankdaler—$\frac{1}{2}$ speciedaler (S) 1826–39. Head right, side whiskers	6–	15–
*327.	32 Rigsbankskillings (S) 1818, 20. Crowned monogram. Rev. Value	7.50	20–
328.	16 Rigsbankskillings—$\frac{1}{12}$ speciedaler (S)1816–18,31,39	4.50	10–
329.	8 Rigsbankskillings (S) 1816–19	3.50	8.50
	Note: Coins of above two types with spelling "Reichsbankschilling" were struck for use in the duchies Schleswig and Holstein.		
330.	4 Rigsbankskillings (S) 1836	2.50	7.50
331.	3 Rigsbankskillings (S) 1836	1.50	5–
332.	2 Rigsbankskillings (S) 1836	1.50	5–

333.	2 Rigsbankskillings—1/48 Rigsbankdaler (C) 1818. Arms. Rev. Value	.75	3.50
*334.	1 Rigsbankskilling—1/96 Rigsbankdaler (C) 1818	.60	3–
*335.	$\frac{1}{2}$ Rigsbankskilling (C) 1838. Crowned monogram. Rev. Value	.75	3.50

CHRISTIAN VIII 1839-48

		Very Fine	Unc.
*336.	2 Christian d'or (G) 1841–47. Head right. Rev. Wild men supporting arms	250–	450–
337.	1 Christian d'or (G) 1843–47	175–	300–
*338.	1 Speciedaler (S) 1840–48. Head right. Rev. Wild men supporting arms	15–	50–

*339.	1 Rigsbankdaler—30 courant schillings (S) 1842–48. Rev. Arms in mantle	12.50	20–
340.	32 Rigsbankskillings—10 courant schillings (S) 1842, 43	7.50	12.50
341.	16 Rigsbankskillings—5 courant schillings (S) 1842, 44	5–	8.50
*342.	8 Rigsbankskillings—2½ courant schillings (S) 1843	3.50	7.50

*343.	4 Rigsbankskillings—1¼ courant schillings (S) 1841, 42. Rev. Crown, crossed sceptre and sword	2–	5–
344.	3 Rigsbankskillings (S) 1842	1.75	4.50

Note: Courant schilling denominations were for the duchies of Schleswig and Holstein.

*345.	2 Rigsbankskillings (C) 1842	1.50	4–
346.	1 Rigsbankskilling (C) 1842	1.25	3.50
347.	½ Rigsbankskilling (C) 1842	1–	3.50
348.	⅕ Rigsbankskilling (C) 1842	1–	4.50

Denmark   **41**

	Very Fine	Unc.

349.   1 Speciedaler (S) 1848. Head right. Rev. Head right
of Christian VIII (accession to throne) — 35– / 75–

350.   2 Frederik d'or (G) 1850–59. Head right. Rev. Wild
men supporting arms — 250– / 400–

351.   1 Frederik d'or (G) 1853 — 650– / 950–

352.   1 Speciedaler (S) 1849–54. Head right. Rev. Quartered arms in wreath — 15– / 50–

		Very Fine	Unc.
353.	1 Rigsbankdaler—30 courant schillings (S) 1849, 51. Rev. Arms in mantle	17.50	35–

354.	1 Rigsbankskilling (C) 1852, 53 (smaller head). Rev. Crown, crossed sceptre and sword	1.50	3.50

355.	½ Rigsbankskilling (C) 1852. Crowned monogram. Rev. Value	5–	10–

356.	2 Rigsdalers (S) 1854–63. Head right. Rev. Value in wreath	20–	45–
357.	1 Rigsdaler (S) 1854, 55	6–	17.50
358.	½ Rigsdaler (S) 1854, 55	3.50	10–
359.	16 Skillings (S) 1856–58	2–	5–
360.	4 Skillings (S) 1854, 56	1.25	3.50

361.	1 Skilling (B) 1856–63. Crowned monogram. Rev. Value in circle	.50	1.50
362.	½ Skilling (B) 1857	.65	1.50

MED GVD FOR AERE OG RET—*With God for Honor and Right*

		Very Fine	Unc.
363.	2 Rigsdalers (S) 1863. Head right. Rev. Head right of Frederik VII (accession to throne)	25–	60–

364.	2 Christian d'or (G) 1866–70. Head right. Rev. Wild men supporting arms	300–	500–
365.	1 Christian d'or (G) 1869	750–	1,000–

366.	2 Rigsdalers (S) 1864–72. Head right. Rev. Value in wreath	30–	65–
367.	4 Skillings (S) 1867–74	1–	3–

*368.	1 Skilling (B) 1867–72. Crowned monogram. Rev. Value in circle	.30	1–
369.	½ Skilling (B) 1868	.50	2–

DECIMAL SYSTEM
1 Krone = 100 Ore

		Very Fine	Unc.
370.	20 Kroner (G) 1873–1900. Head right. Rev. Seated figure of Dania	30–	50–
*371.	10 Kroner (G) 1873–1900	37.50	60–

*372.	2 Kroner (S) 1875–99. Head right. Rev. Arms	3.50	7.50
373.	1 Krone (S) 1875–98. Head. Rev. Arms	1.75	3–
374.	25 Ore (S) 1874–1905. Rev. Value	.45	1–
375.	10 Ore (S) 1874–1905	.40	.75
*376.	5 Ore (B) 1874–1906. Crowned monogram. Rev. Value	.40	.75
377.	2 Ore (B) 1874–1906	.30	.65
378.	1 Ore (B) 1874–1904	.25	.50

379.	2 Kroner (S) 1888. Head right. Rev. Inscription (25th year of reign)	7.50	12.50
380.	2 Kroner (S) 1892. Conjoined heads of King Christian and Queen Louise. Rev. Dates in wreath (Golden Wedding)	8–	13.50
381.	2 Kroner (S) 1903. Bust right, dates. Rev. Seated figure of Dania (40th year of reign)	6–	10–

		Very Fine	Unc.
382.	2 Kroner (S) 1906. Bust left. Rev. Bust left of Christian IX (accession to throne)	5–	10–

383.	20 Kroner (G) 1908–12. Head left. Rev. Arms in mantel	30–	45–
384.	10 Kroner (G) 1908, 09	37.50	50–

385.	25 Ore (S) 1907, 11. Head left. Rev. Value in circle	.50	1.25
386.	10 Ore (S) 1907–12	.45	.85

*387.	5 Ore (B) 1907–12. Crowned monograms. Rev. Value in circle	.35	.75
388.	2 Ore (B) 1907–12	.30	.65
389.	1 Ore (B) 1907–12	.25	.45

		Very Fine	Unc.
390.	2 Kroner (S) 1912. Head right. Rev. Head right of Frederik VIII	5–	8.50

391.	20 Kroner (G) 1913–17, 26–31. Head right. Rev. Arms	30–	45–
	Note: 1926–31 dates never released.		
392.	10 Kroner (G) 1913, 17	37.50	60–

393.	2 Kroner (S) 1915, 16. Head right. Rev. Arms	3–	6–
394.	1 Krone (S) 1915, 16	1.50	3–

395.	25 Ore (S) 1913–19. Crowned monogram. Rev. Value	.30	.60
*396.	25 Ore (CN) 1920–22	.35	.75
397.	10 Ore (S) 1914–19	.25	.50
398.	10 Ore (CN) 1920–23	.30	.60
*399.	5 Ore (B) 1913–23	.25	.50
400.	5 Ore (I) 1918, 19	.60	1.50

		Very Fine	Unc.
401.	2 Ore (B) 1913–23	.15	.30
402.	2 Ore (I) 1918, 19	.40	1–
403.	1 Ore (B) 1913–23	.15	.30
404.	1 Ore (I) 1918, 19	.30	1–

405.	2 Kroner (S) 1923. Conjoined heads of King Christian and Queen Alexandrine. Rev. Arms (Silver Wedding)	5–	10–

*406.	2 Kroner (AB) 1924–41. Crowned monograms. Rev. Crown	1.25	2.50
407.	1 Krone (AB) 1924–41	.75	1.50
*408.	½ Krone (AB) 1924–40	1–	2–

*409.	25 Ore (CN) 1924–40, 46, 47. Crowned monogram. Rev. Value (center hole planchet)	.25	.50
410.	25 Ore (Z) 1941–45	.45	.85
411.	10 Ore (CN) 1924–41, 46, 47	.20	.35
412.	10 Ore (Z) 1941–45	.35	.75
*413.	5 Ore (B) 1927–40	.20	.35
414.	2 Ore (B) 1926–40	.15	.25
415.	1 Ore (B) 1926–40	.10	.20

Note: 1941 25-, 10-, 5-, 2- and 1-ore pieces without mint marks and initials were struck in London during World War II for use in the Faeroe Islands.

416.   2 Kroner (S) 1930. Head right. Rev. Wild men supporting arms (60th birthday)   5–   8.50

417.   2 Kroner (S) 1937. Rev. Arms and dates (25th year of reign)   5–   7.50

*418.   1 Krone (AB) 1942–47. Head right. Rev. Value   .75   1.25
419.   5 Ore (A) 1941; (Z) 42–45. Crowned monogram. Rev. Value   .25   .60
420.   2 Ore (A) 1941; (Z) 42–47   .20   .35
421.   1 Ore (Z) 1941–46   .15   .25

422.   2 Kroner (S) 1945. Head right. Rev. Dates and inscription, *One with his Family in Sorrow or in Victory* (75th birthday)   6–   7.50

Denmark   **49**

		Very Fine	Unc.
*423.	2 Kroner (AB) 1947–59. Head right. Rev. Arms (3 lions)	.60	1–
424.	1 Krone (AB) 1947–59	.30	.50

| 425. | 2 Kroner (S) 1953. Conjoined heads of King Frederik and Queen Ingrid. Rev. Map of Greenland | 3.50 | 6– |

Note: Sold at a premium in Denmark and Greenland to raise funds to fight tuberculosis in Greenland.

*426.	5 Kroner (CN) 1960–. Head right. Rev. Quartered arms	1.25	2–
427.	1 Krone (CN) 1960–		.40
428.	25 Ore (CN) 1948–60. Crowned monogram. Rev. Value	.10	.25
*429.	25 Ore (CN) 1961–66. Rev. Value in wreath	.10	.20
*430.	25 Ore (CN) 1967–. Rev. Value (center hole)		.20

		Very Fine	Unc.
*431.	10 Ore (N) 1948–60. Rev. Value	.10	.20
432.	10 Ore (CN) 1960–		.15
433.	5 Ore (Z) 1950–59	.10	.15
*434.	5 Ore (B) 1960–		.10
435.	2 Ore (Z) 1948–		.10
436.	1 Ore (Z) 1948–		.10

437.	2 Kroner (S) 1958. Head right. Rev. Head of Princess Margrethe (18th birthday)	3.50	7.50

438.	5 Kroner (S) 1960. Conjoined heads of King and Queen. Rev. Crowned monograms (Silver Wedding)	3.50	6–

439.	5 Kroner (S) 1964. Head right. Rev. Head of Princess Anne-Marie (Wedding)	2–	3.50

	Very Fine	Unc.

440. 10 Kroner (S) 1967. Head right. Rev. Conjoined
heads of Princess Margrethe and Prince Henrik
(Wedding)   3–   5–

441. 10 Kroner (S) 1967. Head right. Rev. Head of
Princess Benedikte (Wedding)   3–   5–

NORWAY

CHRISTIAN III 1534-59

		Very Good	Very Fine
1.	1 Gulden (S) 1546. Half-length figure of King. Rev. Arms—crowned lion rampant, with battle-axe	85–	275–

*2.	1 Mark (S) 1543–46. Arms. Rev. Value	Very rare
3.	1 Skilling (S) 1543, 46	Very rare

FREDERIK II 1559–1588

4.	1 Hvid (S) 1575. Crowned monogram. Rev. Arms	5–	10–

* *Indicates coin or coins illustrated*

BENEDICTO DOMINI DIVITES FACIT—*The Blessing of the Lord Brings Riches*

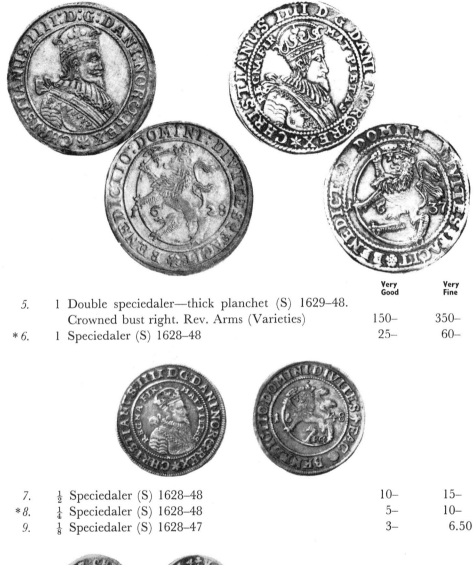

		Very Good	Very Fine
5.	1 Double speciedaler—thick planchet (S) 1629–48. Crowned bust right. Rev. Arms (Varieties)	150–	350–
6.	1 Speciedaler (S) 1628–48	25–	60–

7.	$\frac{1}{2}$ Speciedaler (S) 1628–48	10–	15–
8.	$\frac{1}{4}$ Speciedaler (S) 1628–48	5–	10–
9.	$\frac{1}{8}$ Speciedaler (S) 1628–47	3–	6.50

10.	8 Skillings (S) 1641–44. Arms. Rev. Value	3–	5–
11.	4 Skillings (S) 1641–43	3–	5–
12.	2 Skillings (S) 1641–48	2.50	4.50
13.	1 Skilling (S) 1643–48	2–	3.50

FREDERIK III 1648–1670

DOMINUS PROVIDEBIT—*The Lord Will Provide*

		Very Fine
14.	1 Ducat (G) 1660. Crowned bust right. Rev. Arms	Very rare
*15.	1 Ducat (G) 1665, 69. Laureate bust right. Rev. Arms	1,000–
*16.	½ Ducat (G) 1666, N.D.	750–

		Very Good	Very Fine
*17.	1 Double speciedaler—thick planchet (S) 1649–68. Crowned bust right. Rev. Arms (Varieties)	125–	300–
*18.	1 Speciedaler (S) 1649–69. Crowned bust or laureate bust right	40–	135–
19.	½ Speciedaler (S) 1649–69	10–	25–
* 20.	¼ Speciedaler (S) 1649–63	7.50	15–
* 21.	⅛ Speciedaler—12 skillings (S) 1649–65	5–	10–

		Very Good	Very Fine
*22.	4 Marks—1 krone (S) 1669. Crowned monogram. Rev. Arms	20–	40–
*23.	2 Marks (S) 1649–69	10–	25–
24.	1 Mark (S) 1648–69	7.50	15–
*25.	8 Skillings (S) 1649–68	5–	10–

*26.	2 Skillings (S) 1649–70. Arms. Rev. Value	3.50	7.50
27.	1 Skilling (S) 1649–70	2.50	5–

CHRISTIAN V 1670–99

PIETATE ET IUSTITIA—*Piety and Justice*

28.	½ Ducat (G) N.D. Laureate head right. Rev. Arms	500–

		Very Good	Very Fine
29.	1 Double speciedaler—thick planchet (S) 1670–80. Laureate bust right. Rev. Arms	200–	500–
30.	1 Speciedaler (S) 1670–80	40–	85–
31.	½ Speciedaler (S) 1671–74	15–	35–
32.	¼ Speciedaler (S) 1671, 75	35–	100–
33.	12 Skillings—⅛ speciedaler (S) 1671	10–	20–

		Very Good	Very Fine
34.	4 Marks—1 krone (S) 1670–95. Crowned monogram. Rev. Arms	25–	50–
35.	2 Marks (S) 1670–85	5–	10–
36.	16 Skillings—1 mark (S) 1670–86	4–	7.50
37.	8 Skillings (S) 1670–89	3.50	6.50
38.	2 Skillings (S) 1673–86	3–	5–

		Very Good	Very Fine
39.	2 Skillings (S) 1670–83. Arms. Rev. Value	2–	4.50
40.	1 Skilling (S) 1670–82	1.50	3.50
41.	½ Skilling (S) 1676, 82	1.50	3–

Norway

		Very Good	Very Fine
*42.	4 Marks—1 krone (S) 1686–99. Crowned monograms. Rev. Arms	20–	45–
43.	2 Marks (S) 1686–99	6.50	12.50
44.	1 Mark (S) 1686–99	5–	10–
*45.	2 Skillings (S) 1686–99	2–	3.50

FREDERIK IV 1699–1730

46.	6 Marks—1 reisedaler or "travel dollar" (S) 1704. Armored bust right. Rev. Norwegian lion and inscription, *Courage, Loyalty, Bravery and All That Gives Honor, Can the Whole World Learn among the Mountains of Norway*	60–	150–

Note: Struck in Denmark to pay for King's travel in Norway.

47.	8 Skillings (S) 1727–30. Arms. Rev. Value	3.50	8.50
*48.	2 Skillings (S) 1700–25. Crowned monograms. Rev. Arms	2.50	6–

CHRISTIAN VI 1730–46

		Very Good	Very Fine
49.	6 Marks—1 reisedaler or "travel dollar" (S) 1732, 33. Armored bust right. Rev. Norwegian lion	60–	150–

Note: Struck in Denmark to pay for King's travel in Norway.

50.	4 Marks—1 krone (S) 1736. Crowned monograms. Rev. Arms	25–	65–
*51.	24 Skillings (S) 1734–46	3–	8.50
52.	8 Skillings (S) 1730–35. Arms. Rev. Value	2.50	6.50
53.	2 Skillings (S) 1742–45. Crowned monograms. Rev. Arms	2–	4–

FREDERIK V 1746–66

PRUDENTIA ET CONSTANTIA—*Wisdom and Steadfastness*

54.	6 Marks—1 reisedaler or "travel dollar" (S) 1749. Bust right. Rev. Norwegian lion and inscription. *Obedience to the Law, Courage and All That Wins the Favor of the Danish King, One Finds among the Men and Mountains of Norway*	60–	125–

Note: Struck in Denmark to pay for King's travel in Norway.

			Very Good	Very Fine
*55.	1 Speciedaler (S) 1765. Head right. Rev. Arms		45–	100–
56.	24 Skillings (S) 1746–65. Crowned monograms. Rev. Arms		3–	7.50
57.	2 Skillings (S) 1747–64		1.50	3–

CHRISTIAN VII 1766–1808

GLORIA EX AMORE PATRIAE—*Glory from Love of Country*

*58.	1 Speciedaler (S) 1767–68. Crowned monograms. Rev. Arms	35–	85–
59.	24 Skillings (S) 1767–88	3–	6.50
60.	1 Albert daler (S) 1781–96. Wild man supporting Danish arms. Rev. Crowned Norwegian arms (see Denmark #277)		

61.

	Very Good	Very Fine
61. 1 Reisedaler or "travel dollar" (S) 1788. Bust right. Rev. Norwegian lion and inscription, *Unmovable as the high Dovres Mountains Stand the Loyalty, Courage and Power of the Sons of Norway*	50–	125–

Note: Struck in Denmark to pay for the King's travel in Norway.

FREDERIK VI 1808–14

Note: Coins struck at Kongsberg, Norway (crossed hammers mintmark) during this reign do not carry distinctive Norwegian designs and are included with the issues of Denmark.

CARL XIII 1814–18

	Fine	Ext. Fine
62. 8 Skillings—1/15 speciedaler (S) 1817. Arms. Rev. Value	2.50	5–
63. 1 Skilling (C) 1816	.60	1–

CARL XIV JOHAN 1818–44

64. 1 Speciedaler (S) 1819–24. Head right. Rev. Arms	27.50	50–
65. ½ Speciedaler—60 Skillings (S) 1819–24	10–	17.50

			Fine	Ext. Fine
*66.	24 Skillings (S) 1819 (large planchet); 23, 24 (small planchet). Arms. Rev. Value		4–	7.50
67.	8 Skillings (S) 1819		2.50	4–
68.	4 Skillings (S) 1825		2–	3.50
69.	2 Skillings (S) 1825		1–	2–
*70.	2 Skillings (C) 1822–34		.75	1.50
71.	1 Skilling (C) 1819–34		.45	.85

*72.	1 Speciedaler (S) 1826–36. Draped bust right. Rev. Arms	25–	45–
73.	½ Speciedaler—60 skillings (S) 1827–36	10–	17.50
74.	24 Skillings (S) 1825–36	5–	8.50
*75.	8 Skillings (S) 1825, 27	3–	5–

*76.	1 Speciedaler (S) 1844. Rev. Arms within wreath	30–	50–
77.	½ Speciedaler (S) 1844	8.50	15–
78.	4 Skillings (S) 1842. Rev. Value	2–	3.50

79.	2 Skillings (S) 1842, 43. Crowned monogram. Rev. Value	.85	1.50
80.	½ Skilling (C) 1839–41. Arms	.50	1–

OSCAR I 1844–59

RET OG SANDHED—*Justice and Truth*

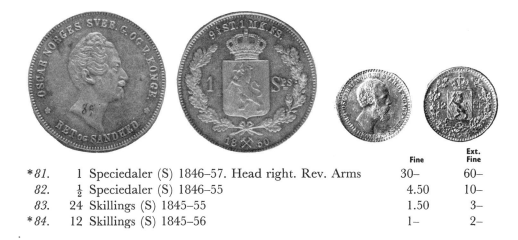

		Fine	Ext. Fine
*81.	1 Speciedaler (S) 1846–57. Head right. Rev. Arms	30–	60–
82.	½ Speciedaler (S) 1846–55	4.50	10–
83.	24 Skillings (S) 1845–55	1.50	3–
*84.	12 Skillings (S) 1845–56	1–	2–

CARL XV 1859–72

LAND SKALL MED LOV BYGGES—*The Country Shall Be Built on the Law*

*85.	1 Speciedaler (S) 1861, 62; (larger head) 1864–69. Head right. Rev. Arms	25–	45–
86.	½ Speciedaler (S) 1861, 62; (larger head) 1865	12.50	20–
87.	24 Skillings (S) 1861, 62; (larger head) 1865	5–	10–
88.	12 Skillings (S) 1861, 62; (larger head) 1865	2–	3.50

		Fine	Ext. Fine
*89.	4 Skillings (S) 1871. Arms. Rev. Value	1.50	3–
90.	3 Skillings (S) 1868, 69	1–	2–
91.	2 Skillings (S) 1870–71	.75	1.50
*92.	½ Skilling (C) 1863	1.50	3–

*93.	1 Skilling (B) 1870. Rev. Value in circle	.75	1.50
94.	½ Skilling (B) 1867	.60	1.25

OSCAR II 1872–1905

BRODERFOLKENES VEL—*Prosperity of the Brother Countries*

*95.	½ Speciedaler (S) 1873. Head right. Rev. Arms	60–	100–
96.	12 Skillings (S) 1873	2–	3.50
*97.	3 Skillings (S) 1872, 73. Arms. Rev. Value	1–	1.50

TRANSITIONAL COINAGE

98.	20 Kroner—5 speciedalers (G) 1874, 75. Head right. Rev. Arms	35–	50–
99.	10 Kroner—2½ speciedalers (G) 1874	30–	50–

		Fine	Ext. Fine
*100.	1 Krone—30 skillings (S) 1875. Head left	5–	10–
101.	50 Ore—15 skillings (S) 1874, 75	4–	7.50
*102.	10 Ore—3 skillings (S) 1874, 75. Arms. Rev. Value	.50	1–

DECIMAL KRONER COINAGE

103.	20 Kroner (G) 1876–1902. Head right. Rev. Arms	30–	55–
104.	10 Kroner (G) 1877, 1902	25–	50–

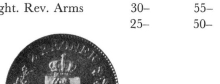

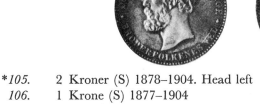
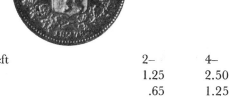

*105.	2 Kroner (S) 1878–1904. Head left	2–	4–
106.	1 Krone (S) 1877–1904	1.25	2.50
107.	50 Ore (S) 1877–1904	.65	1.25

*108.	25 Ore (S) 1876. Crowned monogram. Rev. Arms	.85	1.50
*109.	25 Ore (S) 1896–1904. Arms. Rev. Value	.30	.50
110.	10 Ore (S) 1875–1903. Crowned monogram. Rev. Arms	.35	.60
*111.	5 Ore (B) 1875–1902. Arms. Rev. Value	.35	.60
112.	2 Ore (B) 1876–1902	.25	.40
113.	1 Ore (B) 1876–1902	.15	.30

ALT FOR NORGE—*Everything for Norway*

		Fine	Ext. Fine
114.	2 Kroner (S) 1906, 07 (smaller shield). Arms. Rev. Inscription, *Norway's Independence Completed 1905*, in circle of clasped hands	5–	10–

115.	2 Kroner (S) 1907. Type of #114 with crossed rifles on the reverse (commemorates border watch at time of independence)	15–	35–

116.	5 Ore (B) 1907. Arms. Rev. Value	.60	1–
117.	2 Ore (B) 1906, 07	.35	.75
118.	1 Ore (B) 1906, 07	.25	.50

119.	20 Kroner (G) 1910. Crowned bust right. Rev. Standing figure of St. Olaf	65–	100–
120.	10 Kroner (G) 1910	45–	85–

		Fine	Ext. Fine
121.	2 Kroner (S) 1914. Standing figure of Norway. Rev. Arms (centennial of constitution)	5–	10–

122.	2 Kroner (S) 1908–17. Head right. Rev. Arms, order of St. Olaf	2.50	5–
123.	1 Krone (S) 1908–17	1–	2–
124.	50 Ore (S) 1909–19. Rev. Arms	.60	1–

125.	25 Ore (S) 1909–19. Monograms. Rev. Arms	.30	.50
126.	10 Ore (S) 1909–19; (CN) 1920–23. Crowned monogram. Rev. Value	.20	.35

127.	5 Ore (B) 1908–16, 1921–41, 51, 52. Crowned monogram. Rev. Value	.10	.20
128.	5 Ore (I) 1917–20 (wartime issue)	1–	1.50
129.	2 Ore (B) 1909–15, 1921–40, 1946–52	.10	.15
130.	2 Ore (I) 1917–20	.50	1–
131.	1 Ore (B) 1908–15, 1921–41, 1946–52	.10	.15
132.	1 Ore (I) 1918–21	.30	.75

			Fine	Ext. Fine
*133.	50 Ore (CN) 1920–23. Monograms. Rev. Arms		.45	.75
*134.	50 Ore (CN) 1920–23. Type of #133 with center hole		.30	.50
135.	25 Ore (CN) 1921–23. Crowned monogram		.20	.40
*136.	25 Ore (CN) 1921–23. Type of #135 with center hole		.15	.30

Note: The 50 and 25 ore copper-nickel coins were returned to the mint and holed about 1924. The following issues were holed when struck.

		Unc.
*137.	1 Krone (CN) 1925–51. Monograms. Rev. Order of St. Olaf (center hole planchet)	.75
*138.	50 Ore (CN) 1926–41, 45–49. Rev. Crown (center hole planchet)	.40
*139.	25 Ore (CN) 1924–40, 46–50 (center hole planchet)	.20
140.	10 Ore (CN) 1924–41, 1945–51. Crown. Rev. Value	.15

Note: 50-, 25- and 10-ore pieces in nickel-brass dated 1942 were struck in London for the Norwegian government in exile.

*141.	50 Ore (Z) 1941–45. Arms. Rev. Value (wartime issue)	1–
142.	25 Ore (Z) 1943–45	.65
143.	10 Ore (Z) 1941–45	.50
*144.	5 Ore (I) 1941–45	.40
145.	2 Ore (I) 1943–45	.30
146.	1 Ore (I) 1941–45	.20

		Unc.
*147.	1 Krone (CN) 1951–57. Crowned monogram. Rev. Arms	.65
148.	50 Ore (CN) 1953–57	.40
149.	25 Ore (CN) 1952–57. Crowned monogram. Rev. Value	.20
150.	10 Ore (CN) 1951–57	.15
*151.	5 Ore (B) 1952–57	.15
152.	2 Ore (B) 1952–57	.10
153.	1 Ore (B) 1952–57	.10

OLAV V 1957–

ALT FOR NORGE—*Everything for Norway*

154.	5 Kroner (CN) 1963–. Head left. Rev. Arms	1.75

155.	1 Krone (CN) 1958–. Rev. Horse	.65
156.	50 Ore (CN) 1958–. Rev. Dog	.40
157.	25 Ore (CN) 1958–. Rev. Bird	.20

		Unc.
158.	10 Ore (CN) 1958–. Crowned monogram. Rev. Bee	.15
159.	5 Ore (B) 1958–. Head left. Rev. Moose	.20
160.	2 Ore (B) 1958–. Crowned monogram. Rev. Chicken	.15
161.	1 Ore (B) 1958. Rev. Squirrel	.10

Note: Smaller lettering on 1958 10-, 2- and 1-ore pieces.

162.   10 Kroner (S) 1964. Arms. Rev. Eidsvoll Manor
(150th anniversary of constitution)   3–

SWEDEN

GUSTAF VASA 1521–1560

BEATVS QVI TIMET DOMINVM—*Blessed Is He who Fears the Lord*

OMNIS POTESTAS A DEO—*All Power Is from God*

		Very Good	Very Fine
1.	1 Daler (S) 1534. King standing holding sword and orb. Rev. Quartered arms	850–	2,500–

2.	1 Ore (S) 1522–33. Rev. Arms—three crowns	125–	250–

3.	1 Ortug—1½ ore (S) 1528–34. Large "S" (Stockholm). Rev. Arms	25–	50–
4.	1 Fyrk—1½ ortug (S) 1522–32. Rev. Crown	15–	35–

* *Indicates coin or coins illustrated*

		Very Good	Very Fine

5.   1 Daler (S) 1540–59. Half-length figure of King holding sword and orb. Rev. Standing figure of Christ, inscription—*Saviour of the world, help us*   150–   250–

6.   1 Mark—8 ore (S) 1536–60. Rev. Arms—three shields   85–   150–

*7.   ½ Mark—4 ore (S) 1536–60. Rev. Arms—three crowns   75–   125–

*8.   2 Ore (S) 1536–60. Crowned bust   50–   95–

9.   4 Pennigar (S) 1546–60. Arms. Rev. Vasa badge— sheaf   30–   80–

*10.   16 Ore (S) 1557. Vasa badge. Rev. Arms—three crowns (emergency rectangular klippe)   700–   2,000–

11.   8 Ore (S) 1557 (klippe)   600–   1,750–

12.   4 Ore (S) 1556, 57   600–   1,750–

*13.   2 Ore (S) 1556   400–   1,250–

ERIK XIV 1560-1568

DEVS DAT CVI VVLT—*God Gives to Whom Pleases Him*

		Very Good	Very Fine
*14.	1 Daler (S) 1561–68. Half-length figure of King holding sword and orb. Rev. Quartered arms	300–	750–
15.	1 Mark (S) 1561–68. Bust right. Rev. Arms	50–	150–
16.	½ Mark (S) 1565, 67. Rev. Arms—three crowns	200–	600–
17.	2 Ore (S) 1567	150–	400–

18.	1 Ore (S) 1564. Standing figure of King. Rev. Arms	35–	100–
19.	½ Ore (S) 1561–68. Crowned monogram. Rev. Vasa badge	15–	40–

*20.	3 Marks (S) 1562. Quartered arms. Rev. View of Stockholm	200–	500–
21.	1½ Marks (S) 1562	125–	350–

		Very Good	Very Fine
22.	16 Ore—2 marks (S) 1562–67. Quartered arms. Rev. Inscription on tablet	50–	150–

*23.	16 Ore (S) 1562–68. Crowned monogram. Rev. Arms —three crowns (emergency rectangular klippe)	35–	75–
24.	8 Ore (S) 1562–67 (klippe)	65–	125–
25.	4 Ore (S) 1562–64 (klippe)	125–	250–
26.	2 Ore (S) 1562–66 (klippe)	200–	600–

27.	1 Gulden (G) 1568. Laureate head right. Rev. "Jehova" in Hebrew characters	1,500–	3,000–

JOHAN III 1568–92

DEVS PROTECTOR NOSTER—*God Our Protector*

28.	1 Hungarian gulden (G) 1569. Crowned bust right. Rev. Quartered arms	1,250–	2,500–
29.	1 Crown gulden (G) 1569, 70. Rev. Arms—three crowns	1,000–	2,250–

		Very Good	Very Fine
30.	8 Marks (S) 1570. Crowned monogram, Vasa badge. Rev. Three crowns, legend (emergency rectangular klippe)	1,500–	2,250–
*31.	4 Marks (S) 1568–72 (klippe)	22.50	50–
32.	2 Marks (S) 1569–72 (klippe)	85–	150–
33.	1 Mark (S) 1569–72 (klippe)	60–	100–
34.	4 Ore (S) 1569–72 (klippe)	200–	350–

		Very Good	Very Fine
*35.	2 Dalers—broad planchet (S) N.D. Half-length figure of King. Rev. Quartered arms on heart-shaped shield	150–	250–
36.	1 Daler (S) N.D.	1,000–	2,000–

		Very Good	Very Fine
37.	1 Daler (S) 1569–92. Half length figure of King holding sword and orb. Rev. Standing figure of Christ	125–	250–
38.	½ Daler (S) 1573–92. Crowned bust. Rev. Quartered arms	650–	1,500–

		Very Good	Very Fine
39.	1 Mark (S) 1575	150–	350–
40.	4 Ore—½ mark (S) 1575–81	65–	150–
41.	2 Ore (S) 1570–75	5–	15–
42.	1 Ore (S) 1575. Rev. Arms—three crowns	45–	125–
43.	1 Ore (S) 1575–77. King standing. Rev. Arms	7.50	20–

44.	½ Ore (S) 1569–92. Crowned monogram. Rev. Crown	5–	12.50
45.	1 Fyrk (S) 1575–92. Vasa badge. Rev. Arms—three crowns	6.50	22.50
46.	2 Penningar (S) N.D. Crowned monogram. Rev. Arms	25–	85–

47.	6 Marks (G) 1590, 91. Vasa badge. Rev. Arms— three crowns	650–	1,500–
48.	3 Marks (G) 1590. Arms—lion	450–	1,000–

49.	3 Marks (S) 1590. Vasa badge. Rev. Lion (arms of Gothland)	200–	500–
50.	4 Ore—½ mark (S) 1592. Lion	50–	125–

			Very Good	Very Fine
51.	2 Marks (S) 1590, 92. Quartered arms. Rev. Legend		175–	400–

52.	1 Mark (S) 1590–92. Vasa badge. Rev. Arms—three crowns	25–	60–

53.	2 Ore (S) 1572–74. Vasa badge on shield	5–	15–

54.	1 Ore (S) 1590. Vasa badge and three crowns. Rev. Arms	12.50	30–
*55.	1 Ortug (S) 1589, 90. Monogram. Rev. Arms	8.50	25–

56.	8 Ore (S) 1591, 92. Crowned monogram. Rev. Three crowns (emergency rectangular klippe)	30–	75–
57.	4 Ore (S) 1590, 91 (klippe)	25–	50–

DEVS PROTECTOR NOSTER—*God Our Protector*

		Very Good	Very Fine
58.	1 Mark (S) 1593. Arms—three shields. Rev. Value	500–	1,250–
*59.	1 Ore (S) 1593. Vasa badge. Rev. Three crowns	100–	350–
60.	½ Ore (S) 1593–98	7.50	25–
61.	1 Fyrk—¼ ore (S) 1593–98. Monogram. Rev. Crown	5–	20–

*62.	4 Pennigar (S) 1594. Rev. Arms—three crowns	250–	750–
63.	2 Pennigar (S) 1594. Lion	300–	900–

64.	1 Daler (S) 1594–98. Half-length figure of King holding sword and orb. Rev. Quartered arms	750–	1,750–
65.	1 Mark (S) 1594. Crowned bust	500–	1,250–
66.	4 Ore—½ mark (S) 1594, 98	125–	350–
*67.	2 Ore (S) 1594	75–	200–

68.	1 Ore (S) 1594–98. King standing. Rev. Arms—three crowns	15–	35–

KARL IX 1604–11
(as Regent 1598–1604)

DEVS SOLATIVM MEVM—*God My Solace*

IEHOVAH SOLATIVM MEVM—*Jehovah My Solace*

ISSUES AS REGENT

		Very Good	Very Fine
* 69.	1 Daler (S) 1598–1600. Hebrew "Jehovah" in circle. Rev. Quartered arms	250–	600–
70.	1 Ort—¼ daler (S) 1599	300–	850–
71.	1 Ore (S) 1599–1603. Rev. Three crowns	12.50	40–
72.	½ Ore (S) 1599–1602	5–	15–
73.	1 Fyrk—¼ ore (S)	7.50	25–

		Very Good	Very Fine
* 74.	1 Daler (S) 1601, 02. Half-length figure above shield. Rev. Hebrew "Jehovah"	125–	350–
75.	1 Ort—¼ daler (S) 1600	400–	1,250–
76.	4 Ore (S) 1602, 03	40–	100–

		Very Good	Very Fine
77.	2 Ore (S) 1602. Bust right	25–	75–

			Very Good	Very Fine
78.	16 Marks (G) 1606–10. Bust left. Rev. Quartered arms		650–	1,500–
79.	6 Marks (G) 1609. Rev. Arms—three shields		200–	500–

80.	1 Riksdaler—4 marks (S) 1608–11. King standing with sword and orb. Rev. Standing figure of Christ	75–	200–

*81.	4 Marks (S) 1604–1607. Half-length figure above shield. Rev. Hebrew "Jehovah"	30–	75–
82.	2 Marks (S) 1604–07. Quartered arms	35–	100–
*83.	1 Mark (S) 1604–07	15–	40–
84.	½ Mark (S) 1605–07	15–	40–

85.	2 Ore (S) 1608–1611. Vasa badge. Rev. Arms—three crowns	10–	25–

		Very Good	Very Fine
86.	1 Ore (S) 1609–11. Monogram. Rev. Lion	5–	12.50

		Very Good	Very Fine
87.	20 Marks (S) 1606–11. King standing holding sword and orb. Rev. Quartered arms in circle of shields	175–	400–

		Very Good	Very Fine
88.	8 Marks (S) 1608. Half-length figure with sword. Rev. Lion	150–	350–
* 89.	6 Marks (S) 1609	125–	300–
90.	4 Marks (S) 1608–11. Rev. Quartered arms	30–	75–
91.	2 Marks (S) 1608–11	60–	150–
92.	1 Mark (S) 1608–11	15–	40–
* 93.	½ Mark (S) 1608, 09	25–	75–

94.	5 Marks (G) 1611. Vasa badge. Rev. Hebrew "Jehovah" (emergency rectangular klippe)	750–	1,500–

Sweden   **81**

GLORIA ALTISSIMO SVORVM REFVGIO—*Glory to the Highest, Refuge of his People*

			Very Good	Very Fine
95.	10 Marks (G) 1626. Vasa badge. Rev. Hebrew "Jehovah" (emergency rectangular klippe)		850–	2,000–

* *96.*	1 Riksdaler (S) 1615–32. Half-length figure holding sword and orb. Rev. Standing figure of Christ	75–	200–
97.	½ Riksdaler (S) 1631, 32	250–	750–

98.	8 Marks (S) 1617. Bust left. Rev. Arms—three shields	125–	300–
* *99.*	4 Marks (S) 1613–26	50–	150–
100.	2 Marks (S) 1615–18	75–	200–
101.	1 Mark (S) 1614–18	125–	300–
**102.*	½ Mark (S) 1615, 17	125–	300–

		Very Good	Very Fine
103.	1 Ore (S) 1613–26. Vasa badge and monogram. Rev. Arms—three crowns	5–	15–
104.	½ Ore (S) 1615	8.50	20–

＊105.	2 Ore (C) 1625–27. Crowned monogram. Rev. Vasa badge (emergency rectangular klippe)	75–	175–
＊106.	1 Ore (C) 1625–27. Monogram and arms—three crowns. Rev. Crossed arrows—arms of Province of Dalarna (klippe)	17.50	40–
107.	½ Ore (C) 1624–27. Monogram and Vasa badge (klippe)	12.50	35–
108.	¼ Ore—1 fyrk (C) 1624. Rev. Arms—three crowns (klippe)	15–	40–

109.	1 Ore (C) 1627–31. Quartered arms. Rev. Crossed arrows (struck at Sater in Dalarna)	6.50	15–
110.	½ Ore (C) 1627–31	6.50	15–

111.	1 Fyrk (C) 1628. Vasa badge. Rev. Crossed arrows	200–	500–

		Very Good	Very Fine
112.	1 Ore (C) 1627–29. Quartered arms. Rev. Griffin—arms of Province of Sodermanland (struck at Nykoping in Sodermanland)	10–	25–
113.	½ Ore (C) 1627–29	12.50	30–
114.	1 Fyrk (C) 1628, 29. Vasa badge	12.50	30–

		Very Good	Very Fine
115.	1 Ore (C) 1627, 28. Quartered arms. Rev. Eagle—arms of town of Arboga (struck at Arboga)	12.50	35–
116.	½ Ore (C) 1627, 28	30–	95–
117.	1 Fyrk (C) 1627. Three crowns. Rev. Value	6.50	15–

COLVMNA REGNI SAPIENTIA—*Wisdom is The Pillar of The State*

		Very Good	Very Fine
*118.	1 Riksdaler (S) 1633–53. Facing portrait of Queen. Rev. Standing figure of Christ (Varieties)	45–	100–
119.	½ Riksdaler (S) 1639–52	35–	90–
120.	¼ Riksdaler (S) 1640–46	35–	85–

*121.	4 Marks (S) 1638–49. Half-length figure of Queen. Rev. Quartered arms	30–	75–
122.	2 Marks (S) 1638–51	17.50	50–
123.	8 Ore—1 mark (S) 1634–51	20–	50–

124.	1 Ore (S) 1633–53. Vasa badge. Rev. Arms—three crowns	3.50	10–

	Very Good	Very Fine

125.   1 Ore (C) 1638–53. Quartered arms. Rev. Crossed arrows   7.50   20–

126.   ¼ Ore (C) 1633–54. Monogram and three crowns. Rev. Vasa badge   1.50   5–

PLATE MONEY

    Small denomination legal copper coins were first minted in 1624. A shortage of silver along with an abundance of newly mined copper led to the manufacture of high denomination copper coins produced from rectangular pieces of copper plate. The denomination, date and ruler's monogram were stamped from dies in the center and corners of the plate. Each coin contained full value in metal and the denominations are given in terms of "SOLFF MYNT" (silver money).

∗127.   10 Dalers (C) 1644. Corner stamps, CHRISTINA D.G. REGINA SVECIE; center stamp, X DALER SOLFF MNT (approx. 24″ × 14″, 44 lbs)   Extremely rare

    Note: This was the first plate money coin and the largest metal coin ever issued anywhere.

128.   8 Dalers (C) 1652, 53 (approx. 21″ × 11″, 34 lbs.)   Extremely rare
129.   4 Dalers (C) 1649–53 (approx. 12″ × 11″, 17 lbs.)   Extremely rare
130.   2 Dalers (C) 1649–54 (approx. 9″ × 9″, 8½ lbs.)   1,500–
131.   1 Daler (C) 1649–54 (approx. 6″ × 6″, 4¼ lbs.)   250–

#127 (actual size 24″ × 14″)

KARL X GUSTAF 1654–1660

IN IEHOVA SORS MEA IPSE FACIET—*In Jehovah Is the Fulfillment of My Hope*

		Very Good	Very Fine
132.	1 Ducat (G) 1656, 58, N.D. Bust right. Rev. Quartered arms	1,000–	2,500–

*133.	1 Riksdaler 1654. Bust left. Rev. Arms	175–	400–
134.	2 Marks (S) 1656–60. Rev. Three crowns	25–	75–
135.	1 Mark (S) 1656, 58	200–	500–

			Very Good	Very Fine
136.	1 Ore (S) 1654–60. Lion. Rev. Arms		8.50	20–
137.	¼ Ore (C) 1655–60. Three crowns. Rev. Lion		2–	6–

PLATE MONEY

(actual size 7½″ × 6″)

		Ext. Fine
138.	8 Dalers (C) 1656–59. Corner stamps, CAROLVS GVSTAVVS X DG REX SVECO; center stamp, 8 DALER SOLFF MNT	1,250–
139.	4 Dalers (C) 1656–58	Extremely rare
140.	2 Dalers (C) 1658, 59	600–
141.	1 Daler (C) 1655–60	400–

KARL XI 1660–1697

DOMINVS PROTECTOR MEVS—*The Lord Is My Defender*

		Fine	Ext. Fine
142.	1 Ducat (G) 1664. Laureate bust right. Rev. Quartered arms	500–	1,250–
143.	1 Ducat (G) 1666–69. Bust left. Rev. Cross of monograms	275–	700–

		Fine	Ext. Fine
*144.	8 Marks—broad planchet (S) 1664–67. Bust left. Rev. Quartered arms	100–	300–
145.	4 Marks—broad planchet (S) 1664. Rev. Arms—three crowns	125–	350–

146.	8 Marks (S) 1670. Bust right. Rev. Cross of shields	150–	375–
147.	4 Marks (S) 1668, 69. Bust left	60–	150–

		Fine	Ext. Fine
*148.	1 Ducat (G) 1673–77. Bust left. Rev. Crowned monograms	200–	600–
*149.	1 Ducat (G) 1678–95. Bust right	200–	500–
150.	¼ Ducat (G) 1692	40–	150–

| *151. | 8 Marks (S) 1670, 72. Bust right. Rev. Crowned monograms | 125– | 300– |
| 152. | 4 Marks (S) 1673 | 150– | 350– |

| 153. | 1 Riksdaler (S) 1676. Bust left. Rev. Quartered arms | 65– | 175– |

| *154. | 8 Marks (S) 1692–96. Bust right. Rev. Arms—three crowns | 30– | 100– |
| 155. | 4 Marks (S) 1683–96 | 17.50 | 50– |

Sweden

		Fine	Ext. Fine
*156.	2 Marks (S) 1661–77. Bust left. Rev. Three crowns	10–	30–
157.	1 Mark (S) 1663–74	35–	100–
158.	2 Marks (S) 1678–97. Bust right. Rev. Three crowns	7.50	20–
*159.	1 Mark (S) 1683–97	10–	25–

		Fine	Ext. Fine
*160.	5 Ore (S) 1690–94. Crowned monograms. Rev. Three crowns	2–	.5–
161.	4 Ore (S) 1667–84. Crowned monogram	3–	7.50
*162.	2 Ore (S) 1664–69	2–	6–
163.	1 Ore (S) 1665–97	2–	5–
164.	1 Ore (S) 1661–64. Lion. Rev. Arms—three crowns	5–	15–

		Fine	Ext. Fine
165.	2½ Ore K.M.—copper money (C) 1661. Lion. Rev. Three crowns	75–	200–
166.	2 Ore K.M. (C) 1661–65	6.50	15–

		Fine	Ext. Fine
167.	1 Ore K.M. (C) 1661–64. Arms—three crowns. Rev. Crossed arrows	4–	10–
168.	½ Ore K.M. (C) 1661–64. Rev. Lion	8.50	20–

169.	1 Ore S.M.—silver money (C) 1669–86. Lion. Rev. Crossed arrows	6.50	15–
170.	⅙ Ore S.M. (C) 1666–68. Three crowns. Rev. Crowned lion	1–	2–

Note: The S.M. coinage was intended to contain copper equivalent to the stated value in silver coins.

| *171.* | 1 Ducat (G) 1695. Head right. Rev. Inscription (from Dalarna gold) | 750– | 1,500– |

PLATE MONEY

172.	8 Dalers (C) 1660–82	1,750–
173.	5 Dalers (C) 1674	2,000–
174.	4 Dalers (C) 1663	Extremely rare
175.	3 Dalers (C) 1674	1,250–
176.	2 Dalers (C) 1660–93	150–
177.	1 Daler (C) 1660–91	175–
178.	½ Daler (C) 1681–91	200–

Note: Size and weight reduced from that of preceding reign.

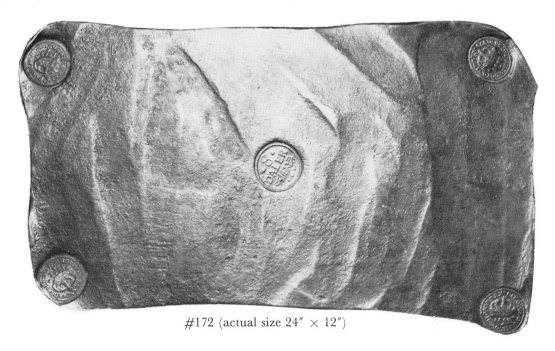

#172 (actual size 24″ × 12″)

KARL XII 1697–1718

MED GUDZ HIELP—*With God's Help*

		Fine	Ext. Fine
179.	2 Ducats (G) 1702, 04. Wigged bust right. Rev. Crowned monograms	600–	1,500–
180.	1 Ducat (G) 1697–1707	200–	400–
*181.	½ Ducat (G) 1701	150–	300–
*182.	¼ Ducat (G) 1700. Rev. Arms—three crowns	100–	250–

183.	1 Riksdaler (S) 1707. Wigged bust right. Rev. Quartered arms	100–	300–

		Fine	Ext. Fine
*184.	8 Marks (S) 1697–1704. Rev. Arms—three crowns	85–	300–
185.	4 Marks (S) 1697–1705	25–	60–
186.	2 Marks (S) 1699–1707	15–	37.50
*187.	1 Mark (S) 1697–1707. Three crowns	12.50	35–

*188.	5 Ore (S) 1699–1715. Crowned monograms. Rev. Arms	2–	5–
189.	4 Ore (S) 1716–18. Crowned monogram	6–	15–
190.	2 Ore (S) 1716, 17	5–	12.50
*191.	1 Ore (S) 1697–1717. Crowned monogram	1.50	4–

192.	1 Ducat (G) 1708–18. Bust right. Rev. Crowned monograms	200–	400–

*193.	1 Riksdaler (S) 1707–18. Armored Bust right. Rev. Quartered arms	60–	200–
194.	4 Marks (S) 1708–16. Rev. Arms—three crowns	25–	60–
195.	2 Marks (S) 1707–17	17.50	40–
196.	1 Mark (S) 1707–17	12.50	35–

| *197.* | 1 Ore S.M. (C) 1715. Lion. Rev. Crossed arrows | 75– | 200– |
| *198.* | $\frac{1}{6}$ Ore S.M. (C) 1707–18. Monogram and three crowns. Rev. Lion | 1– | 3– |

*199.	4 Caroliner—2 dalers S.M. (S) 1718. Crowned monograms. Rev. Crowns and cross of shields	30–	90–
200.	2 Caroliner—1 daler S.M. (S) 1718	12.50	40–
201.	1 Caroliner—$\frac{1}{2}$ daler S.M. (S) 1718	22.50	60–

PLATE MONEY

202.	4 Daler S.M. (C) 1716–18	500–
203.	2 Daler S.M. (C) 1710–18	150–
204.	1 Daler S.M. (C) 1710–18	100–
205.	$\frac{1}{2}$ Daler S.M. (C) 1710–18	75–
206.	3 Daler value counterstamped on 2 daler plate coin (C) 1710–14	500–
207.	$1\frac{1}{2}$ Daler value counterstamped on 1 daler plate coin (C) 1710	450–
208.	$\frac{3}{4}$ Daler value counterstamped on $\frac{1}{2}$ daler plate coin (C) 1710, 12	300–

Note: In 1718 the value of plate coins minted 1710–15 was raised 50% by counterstamping them with new values.

		Fine	Ext. Fine
209.	1 Daler S.M. (C) 1715. Crown. Rev. Value	2–	5–
210.	1 Daler S.M. (C) 1716. Seated figure of Svea, inscription, *Faith of the People.* Rev. Value	2.50	6–

		Fine	Ext. Fine
211.	1 Daler S.M. (C) 1717. Warrior with sword and shield, inscription, *Reason and Arms*	2–	5–
212.	1 Daler S.M. (C) 1718. Warrior and lion, inscription, *Agile and Ready*	2–	5–

		Fine	Ext. Fine
213.	1 Daler S.M. (C) 1718. Jupiter and eagle	2–	5–
214.	1 Daler S.M. (C) 1718. Old "Father Time" with scythe and infant	2–	5–

		Fine	Ext. Fine
215.	1 Daler S.M. (C) 1718. Sun god	2–	5–
216.	1 Daler S.M. (C) 1718. War god	3–	7.50

Note: Because of financial difficulties following the war with Russia, silver coinage was withdrawn and copper tokens of little intrinsic worth were pressed into circulation at their full face value of one daler's worth of silver coin (a denomination actually in use only on copper plate money which contained metal equal to its stamped value). These tokens are often referred to as "Goertz Dalers" after Baron Georg Heinrich von Goertz, Karl XII's Minister of Finance.

(Series continued in next reign)

ULRIKA ELEONORA 1718–20

IN DEO SPES MEA—GUD MITT HOPP—*God My Hope*

EMERGENCY TOKEN COINAGE
(continued from preceding reign)

		Fine	Ext. Fine
217.	1 Daler S.M. (C) 1718. Mercury. Rev. Value	2–	5–
218.	1 Daler S.M. (C) 1719. Personification of Hope with anchor	4–	10–

REGULAR ISSUES

219.	2 Ducats—thick planchet (G) 1719. Bust right. Rev. Quartered arms	175–	400–

220.	1 Ducat (G) 1719, 20. Rev. Crowned monograms	160–	375–

221.	1 Riksdaler (S) 1719. Rev. Quartered arms	125–	275–
222.	4 Marks (S) 1720. Rev. Arms—three crowns	135–	300–
*223.	2 Marks (S) 1719	40–	100–
224.	1 Mark (S) 1719, 20	15–	40–

		Fine	Ext. Fine
225.	5 Ore (S) 1719. Crowned monograms	7.50	20–
226.	1 Ore (S) 1720. Monogram	6–	17.50

227.	1 Ore K.M. (C) 1719, 20. Three crowns. Rev. Crossed arrows	.75	2–

Note: Struck over the token dalers (portions of old design sometimes visible).

PLATE MONEY

228.	4 Dalers S.M. (C) 1719, 20	250–
229.	2 Dalers S.M. (C) 1719, 20	150–
230.	1 Daler S.M. (C) 1719, 20	100–
231.	½ Daler S.M. (C) 1719, 20	75–

FREDRIK I (1720–1751)

IN DEO SPES MEA—GUD MITT HOPP—*In God My Hope*
GUD WART HOPP—*God Our Hope*

232.	1 Riksdaler (S) 1721. Bust right. Rev. Medallions with busts of Gustaf Vasa and Gustaf II Adolf, rulers in 1521 and 1621 (commemorates the 2nd centennial of the Protestant Reformation in Sweden)	60–	150–

	Fine	Ext. Fine

233.   1 Ducat (G) 1720–28. Bust right. Rev. Crowned
monogram   200–   400–

*234.   4 Marks (S) 1720–38. Bust right. Rev. Arms—three
crowns   100–   250–
235.   2 Marks (S) 1720–37   40–   100–
236.   1 Mark (S) 1720, 21   50–   125–

237.   5 Ore (S) 1722, 25. Crowned monogram. Rev. Three
crowns   5–   15–
238.   1 Ore (S) 1720–49   1–   3.50

239.   1 Ore K.M. (C) 1720–50. Three crowns. Rev.
Crossed arrows   .50   1.75

240.   ½ Ore S.M. (C) 1720, 21   1–   3–

Note: Struck over the Goertz token dalers. Portions of old
designs sometimes visible. 1 ore S.M. (silver money) was equal
to 3 ore K.M. (copper money).

Sweden   **99**

		Fine	Ext. Fine
*241.	1 Ducat (G) 1728–32. Bust right. Rev. Cross of monograms	175–	375–
242.	¼ Ducat (G) 1730–40	35–	75–

*243.	1 Ducat (G) 1735–49. Rev. Arms—three crowns	150–	350–
244.	½ Ducat (G) 1735, 38	65–	150–
*245.	1 Ducat (G) 1738–50. Rev. Arms, sun rising from bottom left (struck from East Indian gold)	225–	400–

*246.	1 Ducat (G) 1743–50. Rev. Arms, lion on shield below (gold from Adelfors Mines in Province of Smaland)	350–	650–
247.	½ Ducat (G) 1741–47	150–	350–

*248.	1 Riksdaler (S) 1723–48. Bust right. Rev. Quartered arms, lion supporters	30–	75–
249.	½ Riksdaler (S) 1723–36. Rev. Arms, no supporters	40–	100–
*250.	¼ Riksdaler (S) 1723–36	20–	50–

			Fine	Ext. Fine
251.	10 Ore (S) 1739–51. Cross of monograms. Rev. Three crowns		4–	10–
252.	5 Ore (S) 1729–51		2–	5–

253.	2 Ore S.M. (C) 1743–50. Lion. Rev. Crossed arrows		1–	2.50
254.	1 Ore S.M. (C) 1730–50. Crowned monograms. Rev. Crossed arrows		.75	2–

255.	2 Riksdalers—thick planchet (S) 1727. Conjoined busts of King Frederik and Queen Ulrika Eleonora. Rev. Quartered arms		650–	1,250–
256.	1 Riksdaler (S) 1727, 31		75–	175–
257.	1 Riksdaler (S) 1731. Rev. Arms—three crowns		125–	300–

258.	1 Riksdaler (S) 1731. Rev. Inscription (for King's journey to Hesse)		100–	250–

Sweden

		Fine	Ext. Fine
259.	1 Riksdaler (S) 1748. Rev. Arms—three crowns	400–	1,000–
* 260.	¼ Riksdaler (S) 1748	30–	75–
261.	1 Riksdaler (S) 1750, 51. Rev. Quartered arms	30–	75–
262.	½ Riksdaler (S) 1750	50–	125–
263.	¼ Riksdaler (S) 1750	25–	65–

PLATE MONEY

#264 (actual size 10″ × 10″)

				Ext. Fine
* 264.	4 Dalers S.M. (C) 1720–46			200–
265.	2 Dalers S.M. (C) 1720–50			125–
266.	1 Daler S.M. (C) 1720–50			85–
267.	½ Daler S.M. (C) 1720–50			65–

ADOLF FREDRIK 1751–1771

SALUS PUBLICA SALUS MEA—*Public Safety Is My Safety*

		Fine	Ext. Fine
*`268.	1 Ducat (G) 1751–71. Head right. Rev. Arms— three crowns	200–	500–
269.	½ Ducat (G) 1754, 55	75–	225–
* 270.	¼ Ducat (G) 1754, 55	50–	125–

271.	1 Ducat (G) 1754. Rev. Inscription, "OSTRA" (gold from Dalarna mines)	350–	900–
272.	1 Ducat (G) 1752–70. Rev. Lion on small shield below arms (gold from Adelfors mines—type of #246)	250–	750–

273.	1 Riksdaler (S) 1751–69. Head right. Rev. Arms	45–	100–
* 274.	½ Riksdaler (S) 1752–68	30–	65–
275.	¼ Riksdaler (S) 1752–68	20–	45–
* 276.	⅛ Riksdaler (S) 1767, 68	5–	15–

Note: Some varieties have the denomination inscribed on the reverse, others do not.

		Fine	Ext. Fine
*277.	4 Marks (S) 1752–55	25–	50–
278.	2 Marks (S) 1752–54	17.50	40–

279.	10 Ore S.M. (S) 1751–64. Crowned monogram. Rev. Three crowns	6.50	20–
*280.	5 Ore S.M. (S) 1751–67	4–	12.50
281.	1 Ore S.M. (S) 1753–61	3.50	10–

282.	2 Ore S.M. (C) 1751–68. Lion and monogram. Rev. Crossed arrows	2–	6–
283.	1 Ore S.M. (C) 1751–68. Crowned monogram	1–	4–

*284.	1 Riksdaler—3 dalers S.M. (S) 1770, 71. Head right. Rev. Arms.	35–	75–
285.	⅔ Riksdaler—2 dalers S.M. (S) 1770	25–	60–
286.	⅓ Riksdaler—1 daler S.M. (S) 1770	12.50	30–

		Fine	Ext. Fine
*287.	16 Ore S.M. (S) 1770. Crowned monograms. Rev. Arms	6.50	17.50
288.	8 Ore S.M. (S) 1771	4.50	10–
289.	4 Ore S.M. (S) 1771	3–	7.50
*290.	1 Ore K.M. (C) 1768. Three crowns, monogram. Rev. Crossed arrows	2–	5–

Note: 1 ore S.M. (silver money) was equal to 3 ore K.M. (copper money).

PLATE MONEY

(actual size)

291.	4 Dalers S.M. (C) 1753–58	225–
292.	2 Dalers S.M. (C) 1751–59	150–
293.	1 Daler S.M. (C) 1751–59	100–
*294.	½ Daler S.M. (C) 1751–59	75–

FADERNESLANDET—*Fatherland*

		Fine	Ext. Fine
295.	1 Ducat (G) 1771–92. Head right. Rev. Arms—three crowns	125–	350–
296.	1 Ducat (G) 1771–86. Rev. Lion on small shield below arms (gold from Adelfors mines—type of #246)	350–	850–

297.	1 Riksdaler—3 daler S.M. (S) 1771–92. Head right. Rev. Arms	20–	50–
298.	$\frac{2}{3}$ Riksdaler—2 daler S.M. (S) 1776–80	15–	40–
*299.	$\frac{1}{3}$ Riksdaler—1 daler S.M. (S) 1776–89	7.50	20–
300.	$\frac{1}{6}$ Riksdaler—16 ore S.M. (S) 1777–90	6.50	17.50

*301.	$\frac{1}{12}$ Riksdaler—8 ore S.M. (S) 1777. Crowned monogram	2.50	10–
302.	$\frac{1}{24}$ Riksdaler—4 ore S.M. (S) 1777	1.50	6–
*303.	16 Ore S.M. (S) 1773, 74. Crowned monogram. Rev. Arms	6–	15–
304.	$\frac{1}{12}$ Riksdaler (S) 1778, 79	2.50	10–
305.	$\frac{1}{24}$ Riksdaler (S) 1778–83	1.50	6–

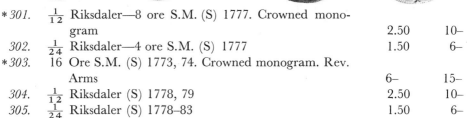

306.	1 Ore K.M. (C) 1772, 78. Three crowns, monogram. Rev. Crossed arrows	1–	3.50

	Fine	Ext. Fine

307. 2 Ore S.M. (C) 1777. Lion and monogram. Rev.
Crossed arrows 6– 15–

308. 1 Ore S.M. (C) 1778. Crowned monogram. Rev.
Crossed arrows ..... 3– 7.50

Note: 1 ore S.M. (silver money) was equal to 3 ore K.M.
(copper money).

GUSTAF IV ADOLF 1792–1809

GUD OCH FOLKET—*God and the People*

309. 1 Ducat (G) 1793–98. Head right. Rev. Arms—
three crowns 150– 375–

310. 1 Ducat (G) 1796. Rev. Lion on small shield below
arms (gold from Adelfors mines—type of #246) 350– 900–

*311. 1 Riksdaler (S) 1792–97. Head right. Rev. Arms 35– 75–

312. ⅓ Riksdaler (S) 1798 ..... 25– 60–

313. ⅙ Riksdaler (S) 1799 ..... 15– 40–

		Fine	Ext. Fine
314.	½ Skilling (C) 1799–1802. Arms. Rev. Value ("contors polett," official tokens issued by the National Bank)	1.50	4.50
315.	¼ Skilling (C) 1799, 1800	1–	3–

		Fine	Ext. Fine
316.	1 Ducat (G) 1799–1809. Armored bust right. Rev. Arms	75–	175–
317.	1 Ducat (G) 1801. Rev. Lion on small shield below arms (gold from Adelfors mines)	275–	50–
318.	1 Ducat (G) 1804. Rev. Crossed arrows on small shield below arms (gold from Dalarna mines)	275–	750–

		Fine	Ext. Fine
319.	1 Riksdaler (S) 1801–07. Armored bust right. Rev. Arms	22.50	60–
320.	⅓ Riksdaler (S) 1799, 1800	17.50	45–
321.	⅙ Riksdaler (S) 1801–09	4–	10–

		Fine	Ext. Fine
322.	1 Skilling (C) 1802–05. Crowned monogram. Rev. Crossed arrows	1–	4–
323.	½ Skilling (C) 1802–09	.75	3–
324.	¼ Skilling (C) 1802–08	.60	2.50
325.	1/12 Skilling (C) 1802–08	.50	2–

KARL XIII 1809-18
King of Norway 1814-18

FOLKETS VAL MIN HOGSTA LAG—*The People's Welfare Is My Highest Law*

		Fine	Ext. Fine
326.	1 Ducat (G) 1810–14. Head right, title "King of Sweden." Rev. Arms—three crowns	75–	175–
327.	1 Ducat (G) 1810. Rev. Crossed arrows on small shield below arms (gold from Dalarna mines—type of #318)	225–	600–

328.	1 Riksdaler (S) 1812, 14. Head right. Rev. Arms	100–	250–
329.	$\frac{1}{3}$ Riksdaler (S) 1813, 14	15–	40–
330.	$\frac{1}{6}$ Riksdaler (S) 1809–14	10–	25–

331.	$\frac{1}{12}$ Riksdaler (S) 1811. Crowned monograms. Rev. Arms	5–	20–
332.	$\frac{1}{24}$ Riksdaler (S) 1810–16	2.50	10–

333.	1 Skilling (C) 1812–17. Crowned monograms. Rev. Crossed arrows	1.50	7.50
334.	$\frac{1}{2}$ Skilling (C) 1815–17	1.25	4–
335.	$\frac{1}{4}$ Skilling (C) 1817	2–	10–
336.	$\frac{1}{12}$ Skilling (C) 1812. Crowned monogram. Rev. Value	.60	1.50

		Fine	Ext. Fine
*337.	1 Ducat (G) 1815–17. Head right, title "King of Sweden and Norway." Rev. Arms	75–	175–
*338.	1 Riksdaler (S) 1814–18	100–	250–
339.	$\frac{1}{6}$ Riksdaler (S) 1814–17	30–	75–

KARL XIV JOHAN 1818–1844

FOLKETS KARLEK MIN BELONING—*The People's Love Is My Reward*

*340.	· 1 Ducat (G) 1818–29. Head right. Rev. Arms— three crowns	85–	160–
*341.	1 Riksdaler (S) 1818–27. Head right. Rev. Arms	30–	85–
342.	$\frac{1}{6}$ Riksdaler (S) 1819–26	12.50	30–

*343.	1 Riksdaler (S) 1827, 29. Head right. Rev. Quartered arms	75–	200–
344.	$\frac{1}{3}$ Riksdaler (S) 1828, 29	15–	40–
*345.	$\frac{1}{6}$ Riksdaler (S) 1828, 29	6–	15–

		Fine	Ext. Fine
346.	1 Skilling (C) 1819–30. Crowned monogram. Rev. Crossed arrows	1.50	6–
*347.	$\frac{1}{2}$ Skilling (C) 1819–30	1–	4–
348.	$\frac{1}{4}$ Skilling (C) 1819–30	.75	3–
*349.	$\frac{1}{6}$ Skilling (C) 1830, 31. Crowned monogram. Rev. Value	1–	3–
350.	$\frac{1}{12}$ Skilling (C) 1825	1.50	6–

| 351. | 1 Riksdaler (S) 1821. Draped bust right. Rev. Medallion portraits of Gustaf Vasa, Gustaf Adolph and Frederik I, rulers in 1521, 1621 and 1721 (commemorates 300th anniversary of the Protestant Reformation in Sweden) | 75– | 150– |

*352.	4 Ducats (G) 1837–43. Head right. Rev. Mantled arms	350–	550–
353.	2 Ducats (G) 1830–43	275–	450–
354.	1 Ducat (G) 1830–43	75–	150–
*355.	1 Riksdaler specie (S) 1831–42. Head right. Rev. Arms—three crowns	27.50	60–

		Fine	Ext. Fine
356.	½ Riksdaler specie (S) 1831–36	15–	35–
357.	¼ Riksdaler specie (S) 1830–36	7.50	17.50
358.	⅛ Riksdaler specie (S) 1830–37	4–	10–
359.	1/12 Riksdaler specie (S) 1831–33	5–	12.50
360.	1/16 Riksdaler specie (S) 1835, 36	5–	12.50

		Fine	Ext. Fine
*361.	1 Skilling (C) 1832. Draped bust right. Rev. Value	2–	7.50
362.	½ Skilling (C) 1832	1.50	4–
363.	¼ Skilling (C) 1832	1–	3–
364.	⅙ Skilling (C) 1832. Draped bust	1–	3–
*365.	⅙ Skilling (C) 1832. No drapery	1.50	4.50

		Fine	Ext. Fine
366.	2 Skillings banco (C) 1835–43. Head right. Rev. Value, crossed arrows	2–	7.50
*367.	1 Skilling banco (C) 1835–43	1.50	6–
368.	⅔ Skilling banco (C) 1835–43	1–	4–
*369.	⅓ Skilling banco (C) 1835–43. Crowned monogram. Rev. Crossed arrows	.75	3–
370.	⅙ Skilling banco (C) 1835–44	.60	2.50

OSCAR I 1844–59

RATT OCH SANNING—*Right and Truth*

		Fine	Ext. Fine
*371.	4 Ducats (G) 1846, 50. Head right. Rev. Quartered arms in mantle	550–	750–
372.	2 Ducats (G) 1850–57	350–	500–
373.	1 Ducat (G) 1844–59	75–	150–

		Fine	Ext. Fine
*374.	1 Riksdaler specie (S) 1844, 45. Head right. Rev. Quartered arms, lion supporters	27.50	60–
*375.	1 Riksdaler specie (S) 1845–55. Smaller head right	22.50	45–
376.	$\frac{1}{2}$ Riksdaler specie (S) 1845–52	12.50	25–
377.	$\frac{1}{4}$ Riksdaler specie (S) 1846–48. Rev. Quartered arms	7.50	15–
378.	$\frac{1}{8}$ Riksdaler specie (S) 1852	12.50	35–
379.	$\frac{1}{16}$ Riksdaler specie (S) 1845–55	2–	6–
380.	$\frac{1}{32}$ Riksdaler specie (S) 1852, 53. Rev. Value	1.50	4–

		Fine	Ext. Fine
*381.	4 Skillings banco (C) 1849–55. Small head right. Rev. Crossed arrows and value in wreath	3–	7.50
382.	2 Skillings banco (C) 1844–45. Large head	2.50	6.50
383.	2 Skillings banco (C) 1845–55. Small head	2.25	6–
384.	1 Skilling banco (C) 1844. Large head	2–	5–
385.	1 Skilling banco (C) 1847–55. Small head	1–	2.50
386.	$\frac{2}{3}$ Skilling banco (C) 1844. Large head	1.50	5–
387.	$\frac{2}{3}$ Skilling banco (C) 1845–55. Small head	1–	3.50

*388.	$\frac{1}{3}$ Skilling banco (C) 1844–55. Crowned monogram	.75	2.50
389.	$\frac{1}{6}$ Skilling banco (C) 1844–55	.50	2–

		Fine	Ext. Fine
*390.	1 Riksdaler specie—4 riksdalers riksmynt (S) 1856–59. Head right with goatee. Rev. Quartered arms, lion supporters	30–	75–
391.	2 Riksdalers riksmynt (S) 1857	22.50	60–
392.	1 Riksdaler riksmynt (S) 1857	10–	25–
*393.	50 Ore (S) 1857. Rev. Value	4–	15–
394.	25 Ore (S) 1855–59	1.50	6–
395.	10 Ore (S) 1855–59	1.25	4.50

*396.	5 Ore (C) 1857, 58. Head left	1–	3.50
397.	2 Ore (C) 1856–58	.75	2.50
398.	1 Ore (C) 1856–58	.50	1.50
*399.	½ Ore (C) 1856–58. Crowned monogram. Rev. Value	1–	3–

KARL XV 1859–1872

LAND SKALL MED LAG BYGGAS—*The Land Shall Be Built by Law*

400.	1 Ducat (G) 1860–68. Head right. Rev. Quartered arms in mantle	85–	125–

		Fine	Ext. Fine
*401.	4 Riksdalers riksmynt (S) 1861–71. Head right. Rev. Quartered arms, lion supporters	22.50	50–
402.	2 Riksdalers riksmynt (S) 1862–71	50–	125–
403.	1 Riksdaler riksmynt (S) 1860–71	12.50	20–

		Fine	Ext. Fine
404.	50 Ore (S) 1862. Head right. Rev. Value in wreath	75–	250–
*405.	25 Ore (S) 1862–71	2.50	6–
*406.	10 Ore (S) 1861–71	2–	5–

		Fine	Ext. Fine
*407.	5 Ore (B) 1860–72. Head left. Rev. Value in wreath	2–	6.50
408.	2 Ore (B) 1860–72	1–	3–
409.	1 Ore (B) 1860–72	.65	2–

410.	½ Ore (B) 1867. Crowned monograms. Rev. Value	4.50	12.50

411.	1 Carolin—10 francs (G) 1868–72. Head right. Rev. Arms—three crowns	50–	85–

OSCAR II 1872–1907
King of Norway 1872–1905

BRODRAFOLKENS VAL—*The Welfare of the Brother People*
SVERIGES VAL—*The Welfare of Sweden*

		Fine	Ext. Fine
* *412.*	1 Riksdaler riksmynt (S) 1873. Head right. Rev. Quartered arms, lion supporters	30–	85–
* *413.*	10 Ore (S) 1872, 73. Rev. Value in wreath	3.50	10–
* *414.*	5 Ore (B) 1873. Head left. Rev. Value in wreath	5–	10–
415.	2 Ore (B) 1873	2.50	5–
416.	1 Ore (B) 1873	2–	4.50

* *417.*	20 Kronor (G) 1873–1902. Head right. Rev. Quartered arms in mantle	32.50	45–
418.	10 Kronor (G) 1873–1901	25–	37.50
* *419.*	5 Kronor (G) 1881–1901. Rev. Value in wreath	22.50	35–

* *420.*	2 Kronor (S) 1876–1904. Head left. Rev. Quartered arms, lion supporters	5–	25–
421.	1 Krona (S) 1875–1904	2.50	12.50
* *422.*	50 Ore (S) 1875–99. Crowned monogram. Rev. Value in wreath, motto "Brodrafolkens Val"	1–	3–
423.	25 Ore (S) 1874–1905	.65	2–
424.	10 Ore (S) 1874–1904	.40	1.50
425.	5 Ore (B) 1874–1905. Crowned monogram. Rev. Value in circle	.40	1.25
426.	2 Ore (B) 1874–1905	.35	1–
* *427.*	1 Ore (B) 1874–1905. Rev. Value	.25	.75

		Fine	Ext. Fine

428. 2 Kronor (S) 1897. Crowned bust left with sceptre. Rev. Quartered arms, lion supporters, "1872–1897" (25th year of reign) — 4– / 7.50

429. 2 Kronor (S) 1906, 07. Older head left. Rev. Quartered arms, lion supporters — 4– / 15–

430. 1 Krona (S) 1906, 07 — 1.50 / 5–

Note: After the separation from Norway in 1905, inscriptions read "Sveriges Konung," the mottoes "Sveriges Val."

431. 50 Ore (S) 1906, 07. Crowned monogram. Rev. Value in wreath, motto "Sveriges Val" — 1– / 2.50

432. 25 Ore (S) 1907 — .65 / 1.75

433. 10 Ore (S) 1907. Rev. Value — .50 / 1.50

434. 5 Ore (B) 1906–07. Crowned monogram. Rev. Value in circle — .50 / 1.25

435. 2 Ore (B) 1906–07 — .40 / 1–

436. 1 Ore (B) 1906–07. Rev. Value — .30 / .85

437. 2 Kronor (S) 1907. Conjoined busts of King Oscar and Queen Sophia. Rev. Quartered arms, "1857–1907" (Golden Wedding) — 3.50 / 6.50

Sweden

GUSTAF V 1907–1950

MED FOLKET FOR FOSTERLANDET—*With the People for the Fatherland*

		Fine	Ext. Fine
*438.	20 Kronor (G) 1925. Head right. Rev. Quartered arms	95–	175–
*439.	5 Kronor (G) 1920. Rev. Value in wreath	30–	50–
*440.	2 Kronor (S) 1910–40. Head left. Rev. Quartered arms	2–	4–
441.	1 Krona (S) 1910–42	1–	2–

*442.	50 Ore (S) 1911–19. 27–39. Crowned arms—three crowns. Rev. Value in wreath	.50	1–
443.	25 Ore (S) 1910–19, 27–41	.25	.50
444.	10 Ore (S) 1909–19, 27–42. Rev. Value	.20	.40
*445.	5 Ore (B) 1909–16, 19–42, 50. Crowned monograms. Rev. Three crowns	.25	.75
446.	5 Ore (I) 1917–19 (World War I issues)	1.25	3.50
447.	5 Ore (I) 1942–50 (World War II issues)	.20	.50
448.	2 Ore (B) 1909–16, 19–42, 50	.15	.45
449.	2 Ore (I) 1917–19	.85	2.50
450.	2 Ore (I) 1942–50	.15	.45
451.	1 Ore (B) 1909–16, 20–42, 50	.10	.30
452.	1 Ore (I) 1917–19	.50	2.00
453.	1 Ore (I) 1942–50	.20	.35

*454.	50 Ore (N-B) 1920–24, 40–47. Crowned monogram. Rev. Value in wreath	.65	1.25
455.	25 Ore (N-B) 1921, 40–47	.40	.75
456.	10 Ore (N-B) 1920–25, 40–47. Rev. Value	.25	.45

		Very Fine	Unc.
457.	2 Kronor (S) 1921. Head of Gustaf Vasa. Rev. Quartered arms (400th anniversary of political liberty)	3–	6–
458.	2 Kronor (S) 1932. Bust of Gustaf II Adolf. Rev. Inscription (300th anniversary of death)	4–	7.50

		Very Fine	Unc.
459.	5 Kronor (S) 1935. Head left. Rev. Arms—three crowns, inscription (500th anniversary of Swedish Parliament)	4–	7.50
460.	2 Kronor (S) 1938. Head left. Rev. Ship *Kalmar Nyckel* (300th anniversary of Swedish settlement in Delaware)	2.50	4.50

		Very Fine	Unc.
*461.	2 Kronor (S) 1942–50. Head left. Rev. Quartered arms	1–	1.75
462.	1 Krona (S) 1942–50	.50	.85
*463.	50 Ore (S) 1943–50. Crown. Rev. Value	.30	.50
464.	25 Ore (S) 1943–50	.15	.30
465.	10 Ore (S) 1942–50	.10	.20

Sweden

GUSTAF VI ADOLF 1950–

PLIKTEN FRAMFOR ALLT—*Obligation before Everything*

Unc.

466.	5 Kronor (S) 1952. Head left. Rev. Crowned monogram (70th birthday)	10–

467.	5 Kronor (S) 1954, 55. Head left. Rev. Quartered arms	3.50
*468.	2 Kronor (S) 1952–67	1.25
469.	2 Kronor (CN) 1968–	1–
*470.	1 Krona (S) 1952–67	.50
471.	1 Krona (CN) 1968–	.40

*472.	50 Ore (S) 1951–61. Crown. Rev. Value	.40
473.	25 Ore (S) 1951–61	.25
*474.	10 Ore (S) 1952–62	.15

475.	50 Ore (CN) 1962–. Crowned monogram. Rev. Value	.25
476.	25 Ore (CN) 1962–	.15
477.	10 Ore (CN) 1962–	.10

120   **Sweden**

478.   5 Ore (B) 1951–. Crown and legend. Rev. Value
         (incuse design—below planchet surface)   .15
479.   2 Ore (B) 1951– (incuse design)   .10
480.   1 Ore (B) 1952– (incuse design)   .05

481.   5 Kronor (S) 1959. Rev. Four men around table
         holding Book of Laws (150th anniversary of
         Constitution)   7.50

482.   5 Kronor (S) 1962. Rev. Athena with owl and shield
         (80th birthday)   9.50

483.   5 Kronor (S) 1966. Head left. Rev. Inscription on
         tablet (centennial of two-chamber system of
         Parliament)   3–

Sweden   **121**

FINLAND

ALEXANDER II 1855–1881

			Fine	Ext. Fine
1.	20	Markkaa (G) 1878–80. Imperial Russian eagle with Finnish arms, rampant lion holding sword, on breast. Rev. Value in circle	45–	85–
2.	10	Markkaa (G) 1878, 79	30–	65–

*3.	2	Markkaa (S) 1865–74. Rev. Value in wreath	6–	15–
4.	1	Markka (S) 1864–74	2.50	6.50
*5.	50	Pennia (S) 1864–76	1.50	3.50
6.	25	Pennia (S) 1865–76	1–	2.50

*7.	10	Pennia (C) 1865–76. Crowned monogram	2–	5–
*8.	5	Pennia (C) 1865–75	1.25	3–
9.	1	Penni (C) 1864–76	1–	2.50

ALEXANDER III 1881-1894

			Fine	Ext. Fine
*10.	20 Markkaa (G) 1891. Imperial Russian eagle with Finnish arms, rampant lion holding sword, on breast. Rev. Value in circle		50–	100–
*11.	10 Markkaa (G) 1881, 82		30–	55–
12.	1 Markka (S) 1890–93. Rev. Value in wreath		3–	7.50
13.	50 Pennia (S) 1889–93		1.50	3.50
14.	25 Pennia (S) 1889–94		1–	2.50

		Fine	Ext. Fine
*15.	10 Pennia (C) 1889–91. Crowned monogram	3.50	7.50
16.	5 Pennia (C) 1888–92	1.50	3.50
17.	1 Penni (C) 1882–94	.75	2–

NICHOLAS II 1894-1917

		Fine	Ext. Fine
*18.	20 Markkaa (G) 1903–13. Imperial Russian eagle with Finnish arms, rampant lion holding sword, on breast. Rev. Value in circle	40–	75–
*19.	10 Markkaa (G) 1904, 05, 13	30–	50–
20.	2 Markkaa (S) 1905–07. Rev. Value in wreath	7.50	20–
21.	1 Markka (S) 1907–15	4–	10–
22.	50 Pennia (S) 1907–17	1.25	2.50
23.	25 Pennia (S) 1897–1917	.75	1.50
24.	10 Pennia (C) 1895–1917. Crowned monogram	1.50	3–
25.	5 Pennia (C) 1896–1917	.75	2–
26.	1 Penni (C) 1895–1916	.50	1.50

REVOLUTIONARY PERIOD 1917, 1918

			Fine	Ext. Fine
27.	50	Pennia (S) 1917. Double headed eagle without crown with Finnish arms, rampant lion holding sword, on breast. Rev. Value in wreath	3.50	7.50
*28.	25	Pennia (S) 1917	2.50	5–
*29.	10	Pennia (C) 1917	4.50	10–
*30.	5	Pennia (C) 1917, 18	3.50	8.50
31.	1	Penni (C) 1917	2.50	6.50

Note: Above coins issued by the White, official government.

32.	5	Pennia (C) 1918. Trumpets and banner in wreath. Rev. Value	12.50	25–

Note: Issued by the Red, Communist government.

REPUBLIC 1918–

*33.	200	Markkaa (G) 1926. Arms—rampant lion on sword. Rev. Value	175–	275–
34.	100	Markkaa (G) 1926	150–	250–
*35.	20	Markkaa (AB) 1931–39	2–	6–
36.	10	Markkaa (AB) 1928–39	.75	2.50
*37.	5	Markkaa (AB) 1928–46; (Bra) 1946–52	.50	1.25

			Fine	Ext. Fine
38.	1 Markka (CN) 1921–24		.75	3–
*39.	1 Markka—smaller planchet (CN) 1928–40; (B) 1940–43; (I) 1943–52		.40	1–
*40.	50 Pennia (CN) 1921–40; (B) 1941–43; (I) 1943–48		.35	.85
41.	25 Pennia (CN) 1921–40; (B) 1940–43; (I) 1943–45		.30	.75
*42.	10 Pennia (B) 1919–40		.25	.60
43.	5 Pennia (B) 1918–40		.20	.50
44.	1 Penni (B) 1919–24		.35	1–

*45.	10 Pennia (Bra) 1941–43. Wreath. Rev. Value (center hole planchet)		.35	1–
46.	10 Pennia—smaller planchet (I) 1943–45 (center hole planchet)		.75	2–
47.	5 Pennia (Bra) 1941–43 (center hole planchet)		.35	1–

48.	500 Markkaa (S) 1952. Olympic rings emblem. Rev. Value (commemorates the 15th Olympic Games held in Helsinki)			7.50

*49.	200 Markkaa (S) 1956–59. Arms on shield. Rev. Value	2–
50.	100 Markkaa (S) 1956–60	1–
*51.	50 Markkaa (AB) 1952–62. Rev. Fir tree and value	.75
52.	20 Markkaa (AB) 1952–62	.50
53.	10 Markkaa (AB) 1952–62	.30
54.	5 Markkaa (I) 1952, 53; (NI) 1954–62. Arms of St. Hans. Rev. Value	.20
55.	1 Markka (I) 1952, 53; (NI) 1954–62	.20

56. 1000 Markkaa (S) 1960. Bust of J. V. Snellman (Minister of Finance in 1860). Rev. Value (commemorates the 100th anniversary of the change from ruble currency to the markka system)   8.50

CURRENCY REFORM 1963
1 new markka=100 old markkaa

*57.	1 Markka (S) 1964–. Arms. Rev. Value, background of trees		1.50
*58.	50 Pennia (AB) 1963–. Rev. Fir tree and value		.65
59.	20 Pennia (AB) 1963–		.35
60.	10 Pennia (AB) 1963–		.20
61.	5 Pennia (B) 1963–. Arms of St. Hans. Rev. Value		.15
62.	1 Penni (B) 1963–		.10

63. 10 Markkaa (S) 1967. Five ospreys in flight. Rev. Construction scene (commemorates 50th anniversary of independence)   4.50

* *Indicates coin or coins illustrated*

Acknowledgments

The author wishes to thank the American Numismatic Society, the Trustees of the British Museum, The Money Museum of the National Bank of Detroit, Jack Friedberg, Hans M. F. Schulman, Robert Obojski and the Chase Manhattan Bank Money Museum for their co-operation in supplying illustrations. Thanks are also due William A. Pettit for his assistance with the manuscript.